I HAVE
WORDS
TO SPEND

I HAVE WORDS TO SPEND

Reflections of a small-town editor

Edited and with a preface
by Constance Senay Cormier

ROBERT CORMIER

Delacorte Press

Published by
Delacorte Press
Bantam Doubleday Dell Publishing Group, Inc.
666 Fifth Avenue
New York, New York 10103

To our extended family, David, Terry,
Lindsay and Dale, with love

Library of Congress Cataloging in Publication Data

Cormier, Robert.
    I have words to spend : reflections of a small town editor / by Robert
Cormier; edited and with an introduction by Constance Senay Cormier.
        p.   cm.
    ISBN 0-385-30289-4
    1. Cormier, Robert—Biography.   2. Editors—Massachusetts—Fitchburg—
Biography.   3. Authors, American—20th century—Biography.   4. Fitchburg
(Mass.)—Biography.   I. Cormier, Constance Senay.   II. Title.
PN4874.C687A3   1991
814'.54—dc20   90-44878
                                                                   CIP

Manufactured in the United States of America

May 1991

10   9   8   7   6   5   4   3   2   1

BVG

The editor is grateful to the following newspapers for permission to reprint their copyrighted columns in this collection:

The Fitchburg Sentinel and Enterprise
The Heat Wave, August 5, 1975
Meet the Bully, April 11, 1974
"God, How I Loved That Suit," July 26, 1973
Christmas—Now and Then, December 21, 1972
A Time for Trees, December 20, 1973
Going Home Again, July 18, 1972
Those Who Don't Make Headlines, October 31, 1972
Beauty That Lingers, February 28, 1974
The Sound of Glass Breaking, May 23, 1973
And That's the Way It Goes . . . , January 11, 1973
Despite the Fun and the Frolic, June 4, 1970
Return to the Bridge, August 11, 1974
Ten Years Ago Today, January 16, 1975
Poetry of Violence, and a Knockout, March 9, 1971
The Governor Visits, March 17, 1976
The Way Life Is: An Afternoon Visit, September 16, 1969
The Afternoon of a Reindeer, January 12, 1971
Beauty Flies Away, September 23, 1975
"Love, The Fantom," February 21, 1974
Ballerina, Turn Around, June 5, 1975
Trying to Convince My Heart, August 23, 1973
The Wrens Come and Go, June 25, 1976
Suddenly, Another Birthday, January 18, 1973
Father of the Bride, March 25, 1975
When It's Time to Say Good-bye, September 14, 1972
Father of the Groom, January 6, 1978
Saying Thank You, June 15, 1977
A Day to Last Forever, May 4, 1977
The Lady with a Torch, November 24, 1976
Las Vegas: Dark and Bright, November 11, 1977
Bar Conversation—and an Ending, July 13, 1971
Musi, the Steward, January 21, 1977
In the Nation's Capital, April 8, 1977
Somehow, You Just Sit There, November 13, 1973
All the Cities We Love, September 16, 1975
Beginnings, Endings, October 27, 1976
What Worries Him, November 15, 1973
Why He's Not Running, September 2, 1977
Wearing Those Glasses, June 2, 1977
Our Food: Too Fast, Too Much, April 3, 1972
The Big Noise, December 11, 1975

The Gum Caper, May 23, 1974
A Brush with Two Goliaths, February 27, 1973
A Few Rules for Survival, December 6, 1973
The Invitation Says R.S.V.P., January 14, 1971
Color Me Green, March 12, 1970
The Game of Us and Them, September 29, 1976
The Invisible Man Who Follows Me, February 11, 1971
The Queen and I, September 9, 1976
Checking Out My Condition, August 12, 1977
"Who Are You?" Here's the Answer, February 16, 1971
The Movie Talker, January 21, 1975
The Film Fan, August 10, 1977
Should He See *The Exorcist*?, February 14, 1974
Since *The Exorcist*, February 26, 1974
Little Orphan Annie Is Dead, March 5, 1976
Nostalgia's Magic at Work, October 19, 1971
The Next Best Seller, August 10, 1971
The Days of Sweet Innocence, October 23, 1973
The Spectators and Some Magazines, August 26, 1971
Many Farewells—A Summer Voice, August 31, 1971
Happily Ever After?, October 7, 1975
A Mountain Voice Echoes in the Poem, August 5, 1971
Does the Melody Really Linger On?, January 11, 1972
Tragedy's Terror: So Commonplace, May 25, 1972
How We Accept All the Changes, August 8, 1972
No Clark Kent and No Rescue, July 16, 1970
The Twins That Haunt Our Lives, February 8, 1973
Keep the Faith, Baby, September 2, 1971
A Small Town Called "Embryo," December 15, 1970

St. Anthony Messenger
The Ghost at Dusk, January 1972
The Shortcuts, October 1975
A Boy Named Pete, June 1980
Sweet Sadness, September 1976
The Cowboy Hat, April 1975
The Signs That Really Matter, January 1974
The Child Who Came After the Others, April 1977
Look Who's Writing a Letter to Santa Claus, December 1976
The Loneliness of the Long-distance Traveler, July 1980
A Bit of Warmth in a Foreign Place, February 1980
The Whatchamacallits Are Taking Over the World, September 1978
The Year I Drove Through the Car Wash, January 1980
Ah, to Be Cool, October 1972

Worcester Telegram
My Mother's Hands, May 12, 1951

Acknowledgment

My thanks to Robert A. Foley, Library Director of Fitchburg State College and Curator of its Special Collections, for paving the way and finding space for me to do the research needed. The columns chosen for this book are part of the Robert Cormier Collection at the college.

Contents

AWAY

FOLLIES AND FANCIES

Preface

IN THE LATE 1960S MY HUSBAND, ROBERT CORMIER, WAS ASKED TO WRITE A human interest column for the *Fitchburg Sentinel and Enterprise,* the Massachusetts newspaper he worked for as a reporter and editor for twenty-three years. He consented under one condition: that he be allowed to use a pseudonym. This would provide him with the freedom to be personal without embarrassing anyone. The anonymity gave him a marvelous latitude, the ability to be outrageous, to take chances, to be sentimental, if he wished. For the next ten years he wrote a twice-a-week column about any subject he chose. In 1973, after three and a half years, the column won the K. R. Thomson Newspaper Award for the best column among writers in the international group that owned the newspaper. Thus, his identity was disclosed. He said some of the fun went out of the writing when his identity became known but this was certainly not reflected in the columns.

The column was entitled "And So On" and was written under the name of John Fitch IV, after John Fitch, who founded the city of Fitchburg. The column proved popular and generated a lot of mail and comment. Bob wrote the column under deadline, along with his other duties at the newspaper. The column was a labor of love most of the time. Readers soon discovered he had favorite words and expressions. *Marvelous, enthralled, beautiful, benevolent, anyway, for crying out loud,* and many more. He wrote of his favorite things. Movies, television, books, plays, music, personalities, family, travel, life itself. Many columns came from his own childhood, his French Hill background, his roots. He wrote many about our children, especially Renée, who was two and a half when he began writing the column. Readers knew her as "that certain child" and watched her grow up. She was eleven when he left the newspaper and stopped writing the column.

There is a looseness in these columns. In his novels Bob's style is tight and economical, but here he could be more extravagant with no need to economize. He has said many times that he tried for the "shocks of recognition." He also had no time to rewrite. He is sometimes repetitious, consciously so, to give a sense of continuity and personal identification to the column. In some instances, he writes about movies and books of the seventies, but many of the films have become classics and now surface on home videos and the books are still available as paperbacks and in libraries.

In 1971, the *St. Anthony Messenger,* a monthly Roman Catholic magazine that had printed some of his earlier short stories and articles, asked Bob to contribute a monthly human interest column. He wrote ninety-nine columns in nine and a half years. Many were expanded *Sentinel and Enterprise* columns aimed at a slightly different audience. In his early newspaper career, Bob also wrote a weekly column for the *Worcester Telegram.*

To put together this collection I reread all the columns, more than nine hundred. Back in 1977 Bob donated his papers and manuscripts to Fitchburg State College. The college is only five miles from our home in Massachusetts, and I was able to spend many hours going through them. This collection includes seventy-two newspaper and thirteen *St. Anthony Messenger* columns. The styles are somewhat different. The newspaper columns were written under pressure of deadline and the others were more leisurely. Because "And So On" was a locally written column, many had references to local topics and people and so were eliminated.

Readers who know Robert Cormier only from his novels will also find "shocks of recognition" here in the many references to his early years—in particular, growing up on French Hill, which is the setting for many of his short stories and his novel *Fade.*

I thoroughly enjoyed my role as editor on this project. It was hard to decide what to include and what to leave out. I loved them all. Naturally.

C.S.C.

"I Have Words to Spend"

I HAVE WORDS TO SPEND AND SOMETIMES SPEND THEM FOOLISHLY, OF course, squandering verbs and nouns, sending metaphors askew, and using similes like fireworks whose sparks often fail to flame. I also have a weakness for absurd alliterations.

There are certain words I love and use over and over again, words like marvelous and stunning and wonder. I've written before about the ember words—there's such beauty in words like September and remember. And then there's cellophane. Cellophane, said slowly.

I am usually attracted to words by their emotional meanings and couldn't care less for crossword puzzles or anagrams, because these words are used simply as devices, like pieces of merchandise. I never win at Scrabble.

Sometimes the simplest words are the most beautiful. And the most effective. Like love and sweet and hon. And what would we do without "and"—the way Hemingway turned that conjunction into a thing of beauty, his every "and" a pearl on the strands of his prose.

But not all words can be trusted. I remember when I was about twelve years old and desperately in love with a girl. Love is always desperate at twelve. Anyway, I'd walk her home from school every day and we'd linger in front of her house and one day she said: "Gee, I think you're swell, but . . ." The gentle brush-off.

The only consolation I could clutch was "swell." She'd called me swell and I walked home thinking how great it was to be swell. A girl had never given me a compliment like that before. And because words beguiled me even then, I actually looked it up in a dictionary and found something like this:

"Swell, noun, a bulge, the condition of being swollen . . ."

And forever after, whenever anyone has said a kind and complimentary word to me, I try to resist gloating over it or using the word as a mirror for my own vanity even though I don't always succeed, of course. Who doesn't love a compliment?

* * *

Anyway, there's one word that is both splendid and terrible and I often ponder its mystery. The word is "but." A traffic cop of a word. A word of terror and beauty. For instance:

"I'd love to go out with you Saturday night, but . . ."
"You certainly have all the qualifications for the job, but . . ."
Or:
"It was a lovely Christmas, but . . ."

But—and there's the magic of the word—it can also be used in marvelous ways:

"I had planned to go away this weekend, but . . ."
Or:
"We really didn't have an opening at this moment, but . . ."
Or:
"The X rays do show a shadow there, but . . ."
Or:
"I'm going to be busy until ten o'clock, but . . ."
Thus it can be a word of hope.

Ah, the words. The fun words and the puns. My favorite pun concerns the ancient doctor who prescribed for an ailing tribesman that he bind his foot with a leather strap. He walked on the strap for months until it wore out. And when the ancient doctor returned and asked him how he felt, the tribesman said: "The thong is ended but the malady lingers on." Terrible, I know, but I love them.

And the malapropisms made famous by Sam Goldwyn, all of them old hat now but still funny, like "Include me out" and "A verbal contract isn't worth the paper it's written on." Old, old, but great.

Words. Words that allow us to communicate, to reach out, to touch each other if only verbally. And the other side of words where we find silence. And how silence, too, is precious. Knowing when not to use the words and holding them back, which isn't always easy. And then arriving at the moment to stop.

And so on.

January 2, 1971

Yesterday

The Heat Wave

I LOVED THE HEAT WAVES WHEN I WAS A KID.

I loved them because the rules were suspended.

If a heat wave occurred, say, late in June, then school closed early for the day. And you were free to scamper home through the steaming streets. Funny—it was too hot to remain in the classroom but never too hot for an afternoon game of Kick the Can or Buck-Buck, How Many Fingers Up in the schoolyard.

The best heat waves were those that occurred in deep summer, when August was the time of the Dog Days and we were cautioned to steer clear of dogs.

Dogs went mad in the heat of August, we were told.

And suddenly, the friendly old collie down the street turned into a threat and you avoided him as much as possible.

The heat wave evenings were beautiful.

The people sat on their front piazzas and fanned themselves with those cardboard fans obtained free at the drug store.

The fans had pictures on them—pictures of beautiful girls or placid countryside scenes. So the men and women sat on the piazzas and fanned themselves, and the women sipped lemonade while the men drank cool beer in the gathering dusk.

Even though it was the Depression, there was always enough money to send out for those two-for-a-nickel ice-cream cones. You'd run through the backyard shortcuts to the store and order the cones, and then hustle back as the ice cream melted, the little rivulets running down the sides of the cones and onto your fingers.

Then you'd sit there and eat the ice cream and there were no flavors tastier than those modest scoops of vanilla, chocolate, or strawberry.

Howard Johnson hadn't yet come along with his twenty-eight flavors and the wildest flavor to be had was butter pecan.

In a heat wave kids were allowed to stay out until all hours. There was no air-conditioning in those days and the only electric fans available were small oscillating fans that barely stirred the air, which only the more affluent people could afford, anyway.

So people remained on the porches into the far reaches of the evening.

And the kids weren't summoned into the house, as they usually were, at twilight.

Dusk would creep into the neighborhood like a gentle dust that took the sharp edges away. Sometimes, an errant breeze would suddenly cool the brow. A leaf would move on a tree. Matches flared as the men lit their cigarettes, small beacons in the night. The summer sky was alive with stars, as if the heat had polished them to a dazzling brilliance. The sky was immense. And if you looked at it enough as you lay on the lawn, you were suddenly dizzy—and infinity seemed to beckon.

The heat waves were also beautiful, I guess, because everybody shared them. Disasters usually bring people together and can even turn a huge nation into a sudden small family of mutual concern.

Every once in a while we'd hear of someone collapsing and being rushed to the hospital with "heat prostration" or sunstroke. But heat waves weren't really disasters—they were something to be mutually endured, and they sizzled the flesh of everyone on an equal basis.

Whenever a heat wave arrives, I hear in my mind the echo of clanging metal—and it recalls the horseshoe games the men played early in the evening.

The men didn't wear T-shirts in those days. They wore those white undershirts that left the shoulders bare except for the straps on the shoulders. The horseshoes lifted and fell and the clang of the ringer was like no other sound in the world.

Just as it was never too hot for kids to play street games in the heat, so it was never too hot for men to toss the horseshoes.

And then to sit quietly later and reminisce and probably argue gently about the Red Sox and the Boston Braves and players like Rabbit Maranville and Wally Berger.

Ten o'clock would come and go, and the evening would advance toward eleven. And magic of all magic, there was still no sorrowful cry: "Time to come in. Time to go to bed."

We'd sprawl on the grass or hug our knees as we sat on the curb and we'd wait with wonder in the deepening night. And this marvelous sense of sharing something together would come alive. I'd think of my mother and father on the piazza, speaking gently in the nighttime, and my brothers and sisters close at hand. The night was suddenly sweet, a time to cherish. I would wish for it never to end.

* * *

Even now, years later, when the heat wave comes, and the humidity is unbearable, there's a small part of me that doesn't mind at all. Because, at some moment in the torrid heat, I am a boy again, and all the lost sweetness and innocence of early childhood is mine once more for a moment.

August 5, 1975

The Ghost at Dusk

HE USED TO APPEAR IN THE NEIGHBORHOOD AT DUSK, AFTER SUPPER ON spring evenings. And whenever May arrives I think back to him, that ghost galloping through the backyards, leaping over fences and springing from doorways, sending the kids scurrying in delight, his face masked but his eyes glowing through the holes cut into a pillow case. His shroud was an old blue bedspread that billowed behind him as he ran his zigzagging course through the twilight. All during that long-ago springtime he appeared, jumping out of sheds or flying down the stairs, laughing, in the gathering dark. And the word would spread through the neighborhood: the ghost is here, the ghost is here. . . .

In the time of forsythia and lilac, when trees were sweet with bud and blossom, when Easter had come and gone but summer vacation still seemed far away, that was when the ghost made his appearance. The neighborhood was a poor one by some standards and the Depression was the pollution of our lives. Wednesday was payday, and if your father had worked a full week someone would be sent to the drugstore after supper for those two-for-a-nickel ice-cream cones. We'd sit on the piazza steps—we always called it a piazza, never a porch—and life was suddenly unbearably sweet. The secret, of course, was this: we didn't know we were poor, simply because we didn't know anyone who was rich.

The boy I remembered didn't want to be either rich or poor but he wanted to be known. He longed for identity and most of all for fame. He devoured Thomas Wolfe's *The Web and the Rock,* reading with painful longing of the young man who went to the fabled rock that was New York and won fame and fortune and the love of jeweled women. He would listen to the radio late at night—the old Emerson in the kitchen near his father's rocking chair—and hear the big bands playing out there in the unknown, fabulous places! "Here we are again in the Persian Room of the beautiful Plaza Hotel in downtown . . ." The boy would ache with the loneliness of those who are unheralded and unsung. He wanted the world to know he existed, that he was there, that he was somebody!

The movies fed our dreams and the boy was, depending on what was playing at the Met that week, John Garfield tossed about by unkind fates or James Cagney shooting it out with the cops while Pat O'Brien called on him to surrender, or he was Mickey Rooney going back to Boys' Town with Spencer Tracy. And always the cowboys— Buck Jones and Bob Steele and the Three Mesquiteers—quick-drawing and hard-riding. The boy would emerge from the darkened theater into the sunburst afternoon, and after blinking away the dazzle, would stride the streets, tight-lipped, à la Ken Maynard, hands at his sides, ready to draw, stalking his way homeward—silent, heroic, no one daring to cross his path.

That's what I think about as May arrives again, that merry and poignant month when the boy, heart thudding, left a Maybasket on the doorstep of a girl who didn't know he existed—a girl so heart-wrenchingly beautiful that he could only worship her from afar. He was invisible to her: she couldn't possibly know that he was Wolfe's young hero or Jackie Cooper in disguise or that the gallant and amorous heart of Errol Flynn's Captain Blood beat beneath his flesh.

But more than anything else in springtime, I remember the ghost who invaded the after-supper hours, the lonely hours of evening when homework awaited inside and you wanted to linger longer in the gathering dark. Your mother called, "Bobby . . . Bobby . . . time to come in."

And you called back, "Aw, Ma . . . five minutes more . . . five minutes . . ." the voices plaintive in the air. Wooden matches flared on piazzas as the men lit their Wings—and that was when the ghost appeared, without warning, rounding a corner, suddenly there—that terrible-beautiful laughter, that flying bedspread, and the kids squealing with delight and joy as they scattered to the winds. The ghost would pause in his solitary majesty, the shroud drawn around his body. The hiding kids would venture forth, tempting the fates, edging near—and then he would explode again into that marvelous laughter and chase them away once more, and the springtime evening was suddenly touched with magic.

How many springtimes and months of May have passed from that far day to this? May will come again and I think back to the old neighborhood and the sweet aches and longings, the ghost who galloped and romped through the backyard in the blue bedspread. The boy never went to the fabled city, and fame and fortune have eluded him. The girl who received his Maybasket went away long ago to Iowa—or was it Ohio?—and he can't recall exactly what she looked like. And the ghost . . . that pathetic bedspread wraith. Had anyone really been afraid of him? Or were those neighborhood kids in need of dreams and drama, too, and were they merely being grateful for the transient excitement he brought to their lives?

As the years go by, you find that there are more important things than fame, that childhood dreams always move away—Ohio? Iowa?—and that ghosts can be lonely, too.

I know, I know. Because I was that boy and I was that ghost.

January 1972

The Shortcuts

I LOVED SHORTCUTS WHEN I WAS A KID.

Never took the long way round.

Never walked when I could run.

Never ran when I could pedal my faithful Elgin—or was it a Rollfast?—from Sears, Roebuck.

The shortcuts were beautiful because they got you from here to there in such a hurry.

And youth is always in a hurry to get there—whether it's a Saturday afternoon movie or a jaunt downtown to hang around with the fellows at the corner drugstore. Or to catch a breathless glimpse of the junior high girl emerging from school with her books in her arms.

There was a beautiful shortcut downtown when I was just a boy—and maybe it's still there. It was a narrow alley between the city's first supermarket—although it wasn't called a supermarket then; just a grocery store—and the Five and Dime. The passageway between these two stores was so narrow that your shoulders were bruised by the brick exteriors as you hurtled along.

There was also an element of danger in the alley. Who knows if you might meet a lurching derelict, clutching a half-pint bottle of whiskey? Or some kid who was bigger than you were and would try to force your retreat, which probably meant a skirmish for your honor. But this sense of potential danger added to the mystery and the marvel of the shortcut. What twelve-year-old boy doesn't yearn for adventure?

Anyway, we'd emerge from the alley into Main Street's backyard, the bleak back of downtown buildings where the limp washings hung on the clotheslines like flags of surrender. We'd run across the debris-strewn terrain and make our way to a brook that slithered like a snake in the downtown area and actually went underground at one point. If the brook happened to be shallow enough that day, we could leap from stone to stone and follow it under Mechanic Street to the spot where it cascaded into a small waterfall where Water Street began. That was a wondrous shortcut—filled with all the perils that a boy's lively imagination could concoct.

There are all kinds of shortcuts, of course, and some of them have nothing to do with traversing narrow alleys and crossing backyards and leaping forbidden fences. They are the shortcuts that youth wants to take to hasten life along.

They want a shortcut that will make them thirteen—and a teenager —overnight, especially when they're just eleven and can't even say, "I'm *going* on thirteen. . . ."

They want a shortcut that will take them instantly from the seventh grade to senior class in high school. To the time when they can start driving lessons. And then having their own car. They want shortcuts to all the destinations that seem so unreachable and impossible when they're only ten or fourteen or even sixteen.

Older people tell them: Take your time, what's the rush, it's wonderful to be young, don't wish your life away.

You want to tell them: Happiness is not getting there—but a way of traveling. You hope that you can bring the old cliché alive. You want to point out that the destination doesn't really matter; it's the trip that counts. The top of the mountain is a moment's triumph when you reach it. The important thing was the long climb and how it was done.

But youth isn't listening to current voices. Youth's ears are tuned to the future and the distant voices that linger there.

Yes, the sweet green time of youth is the time for shortcuts.

These days I want to take the long way round.

I want to linger, not hustle.

I want to pause and clutch the days and evenings.

I want to slow down the clocks, postpone midnight, take a rain check on tomorrow, and make today pass slowly, languidly, sipping the hours like vintage wine.

When all the people I love are gathered under my roof and we tell the old family jokes at the dinner table—ancient jokes now that are funny in the telling and not merely in the punch lines—I want to hold the moment forever, freeze it in time, the way you can freeze a frame in a home movie. But you can't do that in real life, and the moments pass swiftly and are gone.

A while back, there was another birthday to be celebrated at the table. And a little girl whom I used to hoist on my shoulder to watch parades suddenly was old enough to blow out eighteen candles on the cake. . . .

Hey, my sweetheart, don't take any more shortcuts out of my life.

Don't fracture my heart, darling, by growing up so suddenly.

You're not a child anymore and the horizons beckon and you inhabit a country I cannot invade.

But don't bruise my soul by wishing away today when you blow out the candles on the cake, year after year.

You're free to go because nobody can hold back tomorrow. And I would never keep you captive.

But linger awhile.

Don't be in a hurry to flee my premises, to abandon my landscapes, to seek shortcuts to the years ahead.

Even though I myself once took those same shortcuts. And was in such a hurry to be on my way.

October 1975

Meet the Bully

HE USED TO WAIT FOR ME AFTER SCHOOL. NOT EVERY DAY, OF COURSE, BUT often enough so that he became a regular and sinister presence in my life. And he seldom waited in the same place. Sometimes he'd be lurking on a street that I took as a shortcut home. Other times he'd station himself near the drugstore where I stopped occasionally—when I had the money—to buy those six-for-a-penny butterscotch candies or to take swift glances at the latest Action Comics, which featured Superman.

Anyway, there he'd be—my enemy, my nemesis: the bully.

He was older than I was and bigger—bullies often are. He was about fifteen or sixteen and I was about twelve or thirteen. He seemed to be going bald, even at that age. At least, his hair was thinning and you could see his white skull and this made him seem more sinister somehow.

But I could run faster than he could. That was my saving grace. I would encounter him on the street and he'd be waiting for me. We never spoke a word—but he looked at me with such a glitter of triumph and with such malice that instinctively I would head the other way. Sometimes he wouldn't challenge me but merely watch me change my course. Other times he chased me. And off I'd go.

I knew a thousand shortcuts in the old neighborhood and a hundred hiding places. I'd leap over fences and climb second-floor porches and jump from tree to garage roof. I don't think he was in very good condition for running. At least, he never caught me.

Funny thing. We would meet when other people were around and nothing happened. I'd be with a bunch of other kids on the corner, say, or in the drugstore, and he'd stop by and no one would know that we had this secret war going on between us.

It wasn't the kind of thing a kid talked about anyway. Not even to your best friend. All I did was make leading remarks, to try to find out something about him. I learned that he was a school dropout, that he had almost been sent to reform school once. This didn't cheer me up at all. In fact, it made me realize why he had established himself as a threat in my life—he carried with him a sense of impending violence.

I can't recall now our first encounter and why he had started to chase me. And I can't remember when it stopped or why. Maybe he got tired of the game. Maybe he could have caught me all those times and didn't want to—he only wanted to see the fear leap into my eyes.

At any rate, the cat-and-mouse contest came to a halt. I don't know —maybe he got sent away to reform school after all.

He wasn't the only bully in my schoolboy life, of course. I think every kid has the classic school-yard encounter—someone intimidates you and draws you into a fight. Nobody wins or loses those fights really. You are skirmishing to keep your boy's honor intact, and it's the fact that you fought that counts, not the fight itself. Those things are a part of growing up as a boy—and you accept it.

Anyway, anyway. I hadn't thought of all this in years until the other day when Jonathan Winters appeared on a talk show and started to talk about the bully that had shadowed his life at school.

Jonathan Winters is a remarkably funny fellow and everybody laughed as he told about the bully who chased him and took away his new ball or bat even before he had a chance to use them. Stuff like that.

And he said that he had met him years later in life and looked at the bully—and then shot him. The audience howled because Winters was playing for laughs. But I wondered if Jonathan Winters had been indulging in a sweet fantasy there for a swift moment, as the memory of that bully echoed in his life.

It echoed in mine as well, as I sat watching the show. My nemesis disappeared from my life as elusively as he had appeared. And it made me wonder what happens to bullies, anyway, when they grow up. Maybe they grow up to be bullies in other ways. Maybe they grow up to be the guy who cuts in front of others in his car. Or who backs into your car in the parking lot and drives away without stopping. Or who barges in front of everybody else who's waiting in line at the bank or the office.

Or maybe bullies grow up to be like everybody else—or become nice guys after all. Maybe they do.

But I don't think so.

April 11, 1974

"God, How I Loved That Suit"

GOD, HOW I LOVED THAT SUIT. IT WAS BLUE. AND IT WAS DOUBLE-BREASTED, with a pin stripe. It was the first thing I'd ever bought on a charge account. I must have been, oh, eighteen or nineteen, and working for the first time in a big city.

When I tried the suit on in the store, I immediately stood straighter and taller, and I felt like Cary Grant or, maybe, William Powell. I know that dates me, but what the hell. The tailor came over, the measuring tape draped around his collar, and he made chalkmarks here and there but said the suit didn't really need much tailoring, it just had to be taken in a little.

I remember taking it home and putting it on in the bedroom, posing for a while before the bureau mirror and tilting the mirror so that I could get a full-length view. Then I strolled into the living room, carefully casual.

My mother looked up and said the kind of things mothers always say. "It's just beautiful," she said. "Handsome."

I can't remember now where I wore the suit for the first time. Maybe a dance at Whalom Park ballroom on a Monday night in the time when people like Duke Ellington and Vaughn Monroe played there.

But I can remember the way I felt when I walked up the street, the way my shoulders swung, the feeling that every eye was upon me and that I was God's gift to mankind, if only for that moment.

I think of all this now because I came across an old family picture album the other day. It was a rainy afternoon and I was cleaning some shelves. I opened the album and there before me on the page was the yellowed photograph.

It was a family picture, the kind people take on special Sundays and holidays. We were grouped on the front lawn and you can see part of the front porch. It looked like all the family photographs ever taken: somebody squinting into the sun and someone else not looking at the camera.

My mother is in the picture. She's smiling, a smile tinged with pride, and I guess it is pride in the children standing with her. In the picture she is forever young, and it struck me as I studied the photo how she hasn't really changed through the years. Older, of course, as we all are. But her eyes still innocent and the sweetness still in her face.

My father isn't in the picture. He isn't in a lot of the family photos simply because he usually did the picture taking. He'd hold the box camera with one hand shielding the light so that he could see us reflected in the little rectangular opening. And then he'd say the usual funny things, trying to make us all smile. And we'd tell him to hurry up. It's hard for kids to stand still for more than ten seconds or so.

He wasn't the greatest photographer in the world. He'd always pose us looking into the sun, and in some of the pictures you can see his shadow. He's dead now. But in many ways, his shadow is still with us, a sweet presence in our lives.

It's impossible to stop once you start looking at the pictures in an old album like that. The past sweeps over you in waves and the emotions are many and varied. The rain outside is like a curtain sealing you off from the present.

I look at a picture of my brother in uniform. He is posed before the window on the front of the house and a star is hanging in the window, signifying that our family had a serviceman in the war. His garrison hat—I think that's what they called them: the one with the visor—is pushed back on his head in that casual way the fellows wore them on furlough. Or while their pictures were being taken. I remember the excitement when he'd arrive home on a three-day pass, weary, much traveled, and how we'd gather round him, the younger kids in awe of their uniformed brother.

I look at photographs of my sisters and marvel at how beautiful they were. In those days, I thought of them only as my sisters, and sisters were simply that—not beautiful and not ugly either. But now I see that they were really good-looking and no wonder the phone rang in the evenings and the cars pulled into the driveway.

There's also the picture of a child long dead, a golden-haired child, dead at three years old. His memory is a faint blur to me. I was five at the time. My mother said that I always took good care of him when we played outdoors. But I don't remember, of course. I wish I did. It would make a nice memory to have.

And so I leafed through the album and it was sad and nostalgic. I returned to that first picture, the one in which I was wearing that new pin-stripe suit.

The fellow in the picture was me all right, but also a complete stranger. He was the same height but he looked, I don't know, vulnerable, unguarded, violable. Was I ever really that innocent? I wondered.

And the suit. Shoulders too broad. The pin stripe made the suit look a bit ridiculous, the kind the gangsters wore in those old Warner Bros. movies. I saw that I wasn't the dashing figure I had thought myself and that the suit had failed to transform me into Cary Grant after all.

I closed the album and sat there awhile. I guess looking at old photographs is not the best thing in the world to do on a rainy afternoon.

July 26, 1973

Christmas—Now and Then

THE GHOSTS OF CHRISTMAS PAST, HOW THEY LINGER LOVINGLY IN THE MEMory and sadly sometimes, too, because time passes too swiftly, the years like Yuletide tree bulbs burning out, one by one.

I remember the Christmas I was hopelessly in love with a nun whose eyes were blue flowers and whose smile made me ache with longing. The school was presenting a Christmas musical that year and I stood at the edges. I worshiped her from afar, held in the throes of that impossible love.

"We need a tambourine player," she said, those eyes of hers sweeping the school hall.

And she beckoned to me.

On the night of the show, I stood there in a military uniform made of crepe paper, shaking the tambourine. I looked offstage and saw her standing there. And the impossible happened: she winked. My nun. Winked at me, a secret intimate wink that made my heart soar as high as the star on a tree. And that is a Christmas I remember.

There was the Christmas when my brother and I followed Santa after his visit. Down the front walk and around the house and in the back door. We saw him taking off his costume in the bedroom. My father. And that was a delicious moment, knowing finally what we had suspected.

But the moment was shattered by a plunge into sudden loneliness —how lonely a world without Santa Claus. And I wanted to recapture the lost innocence. Later, of course, I realized that the man who was my father was a real Santa, in a thousand ways: all the gifts he gave me, those gifts of the spirit.

My mother's favorite color is blue. And I was a child and saw the blue glasses on a silver tray and knew she'd love them. I saved my money and bought the gift and presented it to her on Christmas Eve. The happiness in her eyes warmed my heart. And it was only many years later that I realized, of course, that in the heart of the Depression I had given her a set of whiskey glasses on a tin tray painted silver, my mother who never held a whiskey glass in her hand. I had seen only the blue that she loved. Looking back now, I realize how much love I was surrounded with, because she pretended, for my sake, that she, too, only saw the blue.

Then there's the Christmas when you fall in love, and the girl calls you "Hon" for the first time. Not your name, but "Hon." Intimate and tender. Beautiful. You walk the chilled Christmas streets together, each of you with one glove off so that you can hold hands in the topcoat pocket. And we still do this in December, at Christmastime.

The years go by and the children arrive and the magic renews itself constantly because you see it all through the eyes of your children. Strangely enough, you discover your own immortality. In the glow of the tree, you realize that the child will be seeing Christmases in the future that you can't possibly see. But a part of you will be there. It's a beautiful thing and sad, too, the way beautiful things are often sad. And you hope that you can be for your children what your father was for you.

Time, time . . . and suddenly the older kids in the family aren't kids anymore and they're scattered here and there at colleges around the country. There are empty places in the house. But Christmas is coming and they're coming home again. You learn that your children have to go away before they can come back to you. The going away kills you a little but the coming back is resurrection. And Christmas is finally the moment when all the people you love are sleeping under your roof and you sit alone at night as the house slumbers, the empty places in your heart all filled.

Christmas past and present. That nun I loved—where is she now? My father, such a good man. My mother who still loves blue, and me. The girl who whispered "Hon" and who still says it now and then, like "Hon, would you mind going to the store, I forgot to get the bread?" And the kids, young and old. Somehow all of it comes together at Christmas.

The child invades my chair, musses my hair, upsets the newspaper, and then scurries away to shut off all the lights except those on the Christmas tree. I demand a kiss. She gives me one that smells faintly of peanut butter. We sit there together. And life is beautiful.

December 21, 1972

A Time for Trees

MY FATHER HAD TERRIBLE LUCK WITH CHRISTMAS TREES.

He always brought home some pathetic specimen that looked as if it had been used to sweep the streets. Or he'd drag in what looked like a reject from the woods.

It wasn't entirely his fault, of course. Those were the years of the Depression and money was scarce, and a man with a family to feed and clothe and educate tried to shop shrewdly, even for a Christmas tree.

In those days, the Christmas season didn't begin the day after Thanksgiving. I can remember December descending bleakly upon us, the biting wind, the first snows. But suddenly a lamp was lit on the landscape of the season—Christmas was coming. Department stores opened their Toylands. Then, the Saturday before Christmas itself my father would go out to buy the tree.

This was a ritual he performed alone, a solitary shopping trip. He'd stop by to see his cronies at the Welcome Bar—how often he and I, in later years, sat in a booth and watched Ted Williams hit the rainbow arc to right field—anyway, he'd stop by there because the bar was a neighborhood kind of place where a man cooled himself on summer days and warmed himself in winter. And got into the mood to brave the elements and go buy a tree.

At home, we'd be waiting for him. My mother would bring out the cardboard boxes that contained the decorations—the ornaments always seemed like old friends. There was no star as beautiful as ours.

And my father would arrive. He always looked triumphant—and defiant. Triumphant because he'd probably gotten a bargain and defiant because he was prepared to defend his choice.

The tree would be shriveled with cold and it would have to thaw for a while. After supper, the great moment for decorating would arrive.

"My God," my mother would say. "What have you brought home?"

We would gaze in disbelief at the tree. There'd be a great gap halfway up the trunk. "Turn it around." And there'd always be a gap on the other side.

But we'd decorate it. "All Christmas trees are beautiful," my father always said.

I remember the year that the tree turned out to be huge and full and we couldn't believe our eyes. Suddenly, small movements were observed in the tree as it thawed. A flicker of action here and there. Something darting up and around—and across the floor. The tree was filled with mice! They leaped to joyous life in the warmth and went scurrying all over the place.

My father wasn't bothered much. "Let the mice have a Merry Christmas at our house," he said. Or words to that effect.

One year, the tree was lopsided—fat on one side and skinny on the other. He took out a drill and made holes on the skinny side. Then he transferred branches from the fat side. He used a foul-smelling glue that forced us to open the windows on the coldest night of the year.

Another year, the tree began to shed as soon as he got it into the house. The needles came down like raindrops, covering the floor, a puddle of pine.

The funny thing is that my father was right—our Christmas trees all were beautiful. Once they were garlanded with the decorations and ornaments and adorned with glittering icicles, the trees were marvelous to behold.

So, I think of the Christmas trees as the holiday approaches and I think of my father. He dressed up as Santa Claus on Christmas Eve and came stomping in, a bulging pillowcase over his shoulder, and he'd pass out the gifts. He was an unlikely Santa Claus: a short, gentle man with a quick dry wit and generous good humor. But he wasn't the roly-poly, ho-ho-ho type. Yet each year he put on the costume. I remember the years I was his helper out in the hallway, assisting him with the costume, and he'd say: "I've got to stop doing things like this." He didn't, of course, until he stopped doing everything.

The time came finally when I wasn't a kid anymore and the day came for me to set forth on a Saturday afternoon to buy a tree of my own. I didn't stalk the streets as my father did—I drove. Price was no object—the affluent society.

Tree selection always baffled me. I can't tell a Canadian balsam from a pine or spruce. All I want is something that will stand up. Anyway, I came home one year and stored the tree in the garage. Then I brought it out in the evening. I had trouble driving its base onto the nail at the bottom of the tree stand. Finally it stood by itself.

The kids looked at it in awe.

Or maybe horror.

It was a tramp of a tree, a derelict, swaying drunkenly, with missing branches.

"Hey, Dad, how much did the guy pay you to take it away?" someone said. Always a wise guy in the crowd.

A certain person who has shared stars and scars with me looked gently in my direction. "I guess it runs in the family," she said.

I thought of my father—that great good guy—Santa Claus in a suit that didn't quite fit one night of the year and a real Santa Claus to us the other 364 days and nights. I hoped that the things he was ran in the family . . . in my own blood.

"All Christmas trees are beautiful," I said.

December 20, 1973

A Boy Named Pete

PETE DIGNARD WAS MY BEST FRIEND WHEN WE LIVED IN THE THREE-DECKER house on Laurel Street back in the days when we attended St. Cecilia's Parochial School. His family lived on the first floor and my family lived on the second. Both of our families were large, and the building was tumultuous with people coming and going, being born and growing up.

Those were the days of the Depression and our fathers worked in uncertain jobs in the shops. Pete and I knew vaguely that we were poor, but it didn't seem to mean very much. We had a deserted cellar hole to play in at the corner of Mechanic and Laurel, we managed to buy occasional two-for-a-nickel ice cream cones at Lamothe's Drug Store, and we seldom missed the Saturday afternoon cowboy movies at the Plymouth Theater.

We were an enterprising pair. We scoured French Hill for empty soda bottles and sold them for two cents each at Lamothe's. We sold soap for "Old Jake," who came around twice a month with his wagon full of merchandise, and earned a penny commission for each sale. We ran errands and did chores for Mrs. Angvier, who was old and feeble and never left her third-floor tenement on Third Street. We also had a lot of fun.

Pete and I never spoke of our friendship. It would have embarrassed both of us. Yet the bond between us was strong and abiding. In choosing sides for a game of corner-lot baseball, I was secure in the knowledge that Pete, who was a much better player, would choose me first. (The worst thing for a kid was to be chosen one of the last.)

I, in turn, never charged Pete admission to the frequent shows I produced in the tenement cellar. Pete, in fact, was my right-hand man, assisting me with setting the atmosphere for the ghost stories I told while wrapped in an old bedspread my mother had abandoned, or helping me arrange the exhibits in the circus "sideshow" I put on one week. (I can't imagine now what those exhibits could have been, but the smaller kids paid a penny admission and no one ever demanded a refund.)

If our friendship ever faced a test, it was the time I fell desperately in love with a girl from the other side of town. She was tall and blond and turned my knees liquid when I spotted her downtown. I followed her home at a discreet distance and was dismayed to see her enter a big white house on one of the fanciest streets in town. I spent several afternoons and evenings riding my bike in front of the house, hoping to see the girl. Her family name was written in fancy script on the mailbox and I looked it up in the telephone book. But I never called her. For one thing, I didn't know her first name; for another, we had no phone at home. In fact, I had never made a phone call in my life.

For weeks I lived in an agony of longing, torn between the sweetness that filled me when I caught an occasional glimpse of her and the desperation that swept me when I realized our love was impossible. I didn't know then that twelve-year-old love is always impossible.

Pete was loyal and patient during this anguished period. He accompanied me on evening visits to the girl's street, listened to my romantic schemes ("Maybe I should write her a letter and say that she has an unknown protector watching over her") and never uttered a word of protest.

Finally I fell out of love with her as quickly as I had fallen for her charms. Maybe it was the lack of response, the boredom of those fruitless trips across town.

At any rate, life became normal once again. Pete and I built a clubhouse from old boards someone had deposited in the dump. I learned to play the guitar and sang cowboy songs endlessly. A Wild West show came to town, pitching its tent in a vacant lot in the neighborhood and Pete and I became water boys, earning our way into every performance by carrying water to the thirsty horses. It wasn't really a Wild West show—the cowboys did more singing than riding and the horses seemed permanently exhausted—but the show filled our days and evenings with a dazzle and glamour that remained long after the last cowboy drove out of sight in a lumbering decrepit truck.

Through it all, Pete and I were best friends, always running, competing for baseball cards that came with bubble gum, swapping marbles, fixing flat tires on our bikes with homemade patches. We seemed to have lived a lifetime in the two years we had known each other on Laurel Street.

Then the fire. On a bright June afternoon, fire swept the three-decker we called home, sending our mothers and younger brothers and sisters to the street. Luckily, no one was injured. Once we knew that everyone was safe—my guitar also emerged unscathed—Pete and I enjoyed the drama of firemen and fire trucks and howling sirens.

The fire signaled the end of an era, however. And a friendship. Our families were unable to return to their tenements, and we kids were placed with relatives or friends for a few weeks. My father eventually found a first-floor tenement on the other side of French Hill. Pete and I lost track of each other. I graduated from St. Cecilia's at the end of June. Pete was a year behind me, having lost a year when he broke his leg in the sixth grade. That hadn't seemed to matter, earlier. But now we lived in different neighborhoods and I was off to junior high school downtown in the fall. I seldom saw Pete in the months that followed. Later, I learned he had gone to live with relatives in New York state.

The other day, I read in the newspaper that Pete's father had died. His body was being brought back to French Hill for the wake and funeral. I was certain Pete would come. I drove to the funeral home on a chilly spring evening to pay my respects and see my boyhood friend. Would we recognize each other after all these years?

I knew him immediately—he was older, of course, and had gained a bit of weight (as I had, too), but his eyes had the brightness I remembered and his quick smile was as ready as ever. We talked awhile and then there were awkward pauses. We reminisced about the old days but the words faltered. Perhaps it was the wake itself and his dead father lying nearby. Perhaps it was the years which can't be bridged. Perhaps Thomas Wolfe was right when he said that you can't go home again to youth and early times. I went to the wake looking for the lost boy I knew. I didn't find him, just as Peter didn't see the skinny kid who had told ghost stories shrouded in an old bedspread.

On the way home I drove by Laurel Street and looked at the old three-decker looming in the darkness. Good-bye, Pete, I said, although we had really said good-bye forty years ago when fire struck the house that was our home.

June 1980

Sweet Sadness

THERE WAS AN OLD SAYING DURING THE DEPRESSION THAT IT WAS CHEAPER TO move than to pay rent. My family was caught in the clutches of the Depression and we moved a lot, from one three-decker tenement building to another, although my father always paid the rent.

In those days tenements were plentiful and the physical part of moving was easy. In the first place, people didn't move far, only a street or two away. Or sometimes across the street: from a third-floor back to a first-floor flat. Nobody ever saw a moving van on the streets of French Hill—friends and relatives and neighbors got together and did the moving, most often in a borrowed truck. There was a kind of carnival atmosphere to it all, especially when the men sat around afterward drinking home-brewed beer and marveling at the miracle of carrying that old black stove up three flights of stairs.

I thought of all this the other day when nine-year-old Renée and I drove through the streets of that old neighborhood of mine. I had long ago pointed out the house where I was born—the three-story building is still standing there on Sixth Street. I was born on the third floor, and Renée still shakes her head in wonder at the event, having been born, of course, like everyone else she knows, in a hospital.

This particular day, we turned the corner from Water Street onto Fifth and I pointed to the corner building. "That's where I lived when I went to high school," I said. "I wrote my first story in that house, sitting at the kitchen table, using one of those tablets with lined paper." Further along Fifth Street, I pointed to another three-decker. "That's where my brother Leo died," I said. "He was three years old and I was five when he died." I remember vividly the room he died in, and as we passed by I looked at the window of that bedroom. I remembered how I'd been sent to summon my grand-father on the morning Leo died, how I'd scurried through the back-yards between Fifth and Sixth on that desperate mission.

We rounded the corner, traversed Spruce Street for a block, and turned left onto Fourth. I indicated the three-decker next to the paro-chial school. "We lived on the second floor there when I was in the sixth and seventh grades," I said. "It was great living next door to the school—you could sneak home at recess. The entire schoolyard was your backyard. And you didn't have to leave the house on cold morn-ings until the last minute. . . ."

"Why did you move so much, Dad?" she asked, honestly puzzled. She has lived in the same house for nine years and expects to live there until she gets married or goes off to be a horse trainer, whichever comes first.

"Oh, a lot of reasons," I answered. When a new baby was born, my father would seek a bigger apartment. Or one with bigger rooms, especially rooms that could accommodate two double beds. We moved, of course, the week after my brother Leo died, those rooms on Fifth Street shadowed forever by his death. Fire ravaged the house on Laurel Street, necessitating another move. It was a mid-morning fire visible from my eighth-grade classroom and I watched horrified as the flames chewed at the house. The good sister allowed me to leave —but only after insisting that we all say aloud a decade of the rosary. I rushed out to find my mother and the small ones safe.

We turned on Mechanic Street, and I stopped in front of a two-story building, not a three-decker this time. A "Beauty Parlor" now occupies the first floor. We lived on the second floor for only a year. But what a momentous year: I went to my first nighttime movie—a horror movie, as it turned out—and we walked home in beautiful fright. I got my first job, doing errands at a drugstore and, best of all, filling the penny-candy cases. The owner, Mr. Lamothe, never seemed to mind allowing a few free samples. And I fell desperately in love with a girl from the other side of town, having seen her at a distance when a bunch of us kids from French Hill went bike riding across the city.

I haunted her street for weeks that springtime, catching heart-wrenching glimpses of her. She was slender and blond and always seemed to be wearing a white blouse. A birdbath—think of it: a birdbath!—graced the emerald lawn that aproned the front of her house. Her house looked like a huge white birthday cake and I later used it in a short story. But I never met the girl who lived in the house. Her family soon moved away, and I don't recall her name now, only that distant ache of too much longing.

"Where else did you live, Dad?" Renée asked.

"Oh, a lot of places," I said, thinking of all the tenements and all the living that went on in them. I thought, too, of the final house, on Second Street, the house my father bought after all those years of rentals. We drove to that house and parked across the street. The house is painted green now: I remember it was white. The new owners have done something to the back porch, closed it in. My father loved this house. He planted a garden in the backyard: his own piece of earth. He worked all those years and roamed like a nomad through the wooden cliffs of French Hill and finally was able to buy a home of his own. He died there, in one of those rooms.

When my father was negotiating the purchase of the house, he would disappear on those summer evenings. We learned later that he'd stroll to the house and sit across the street on a small stone wall and simply stare at the house in the gathering dusk. But he wasn't really staring, of course. He was dreaming. I don't know about his other dreams, but that one dream came true.

"What's the matter, Dad?" Renée asked.
"Nothing," I replied.
"You look sad," she said.

Maybe I did. But there's such a thing as sweet sadness, and it's the kind that comes when you take a trip through the old neighborhood of your childhood.

September 1976

The Cowboy Hat

IT'S RIDICULOUS, OF COURSE, BUT THE FACT OF THE MATTER IS THAT I'VE always wanted to be a cowboy. It's ridiculous because, in the first place, I'm not the outdoor type and I feel more comfortable with a sidewalk under my feet than a woodland trail. In the second place, I've never even sat on a horse and know nothing about cows.

Actually, I've never wanted to be a real cowboy. I've wanted to be like the cowboys in those Saturday afternoon movies that still turn up on television. Cowboys like Hopalong Cassidy and Buck Jones and Hoot Gibson and even Roy Rogers, although I never really cared for those cowboys who interrupted all the action to sing a song.

When I was a boy, I always included a cowboy suit on my Christmas lists. And, more often than not, some kind of cowboy outfit would appear under the tree. I still remember a sheepskin holster that was soft to the touch and resembled the kind that Ken Maynard wore. Another year I received a two-gun set, and this was the ultimate. Standing before the mirror, I practiced my draw, whipping the pistols out of their holsters with swiftness and dispatch.

I shot down a million bad guys without ever firing a gun.

In those far-off days, things weren't as sophisticated as they are today, and I realize, in retrospect, that those old cowboy outfits left a lot to be desired. For instance, the hats were always wrong. Most of the hats had flat brims and the brims were actually made of cardboard that was covered with cheap cloth. The hats never looked like the magnificent Stetsons worn by the cowboys in the movies.

Those cowboys cast such a spell on our lives. The boy I used to be would leave the theater late on a Saturday afternoon in the waning daylight and walk down the street with that John Wayne kind of swagger, moving his shoulders dangerously, as if he were about to burst through the swinging doors of a saloon. He'd take a shortcut across the railroad tracks and imagine himself galloping to overtake a fast freight. He'd run across the field near the church in pursuit of the bank robbers, who'd taken a pretty girl as hostage. Those were marvelous moments—moments of sweetness and innocence when the bad guys appeared only in your daydreams and the good guy always won.

I still get a kick out of cowboy pictures on occasion, especially the old ones that show up on television. I realize their defects now—the terrible acting, the holes in the plots, all the coincidences. But an old John Wayne film like *Somewhere in Sonora* can still lure me to the set, although I'm aware that those cowboy days are part of a distant past.

And then, one day a while back, I found myself in a clothing store. And I spotted, on a counter, a row of cowboy hats—not the fake kind that came with the old cowboy outfits and not an imitation, but the real thing.

Now, I seldom wear a hat because I always feel ridiculous in one. Some men can wear hats with style and class, but I'm not one of them. But that cowboy hat was irresistible and I figured: why not? I tried it on. The hat felt good on my head and I was aware of that curving brim. I shrugged my shoulders, and my hand darted to the invisible holster at my side. Then I made a mistake: I glanced into the mirror and saw this funny-looking man looking back at me. I could do nothing but laugh. And a certain lady who has shared the good times and the bad times with me also burst into laughter. We had a good time as I mugged before the mirror.

But, for a moment there, when I first put on the hat, it had been beautiful. . . .

A week or so later, we were shopping in a new store, a place that specialized in leather goods, and I saw another hat that was exactly like the old Buck Jones or Tom Tyler type. I waited for the others to drift away and then tried it on. I took a chance on the mirror again—and, you know, this time it didn't look so ridiculous.

My birthday was approaching and, frankly, I'm at the age where you don't get excited about birthdays anymore. In fact, I'd rather forget about them. But the kids always make a fuss and that certain lady bakes a cake—chocolate. Anyway, I went to the table for dinner the other day and saw a package near my plate. I was surprised, because my birthday was still a few days away. Then I realized that my son was home from college for a vacation but had to return before the birthday arrived. I saw the look on his face, the eager anticipation, and knew that the present was from him.

I opened the package—and there was the cowboy hat. With that curved brim. There was laughter all around as I put it on, because I'm not really the cowboy type. I tried a two-gun draw. I played the part of a clown for a while: I never mind playing the clown for people I love.

We had a good time that evening and I wore the hat around the house for a while just for laughs. Later, when everyone was asleep, I put the hat on again. I thought of those long-ago boyhood days and the movies, and about lost sweetness, lost innocence. And I also thought of a boy—not a boy anymore, but a man, really—who had cared enough about another man's dreams and memories to buy him a cowboy hat.

I dozed in the chair, the hat tipped forward on my head, and in the beautiful land that's neither sleeping nor waking I was finally a cowboy, galloping forever over the fields and prairies.

April 1975

Going Home Again

"HEY, MISTER, WHAT'RE YOU DOING?" THE KID ASKED.

Going home, I might have answered—but he was gone too soon, streaking by the car on his bicycle. I knew why he was curious. It was a residential street on a melting, steaming afternoon and he had seen the car parked at the curb and me, the stranger, inside. And I wondered whether, even now, housewives were peeking out of windows behind curtains, looking at the suspicious car on the street. Going home.

Thomas Wolfe said you can't go home again. But I wondered. A while back I had driven on this same street, a certain five-year-old child beside me. Passing by a particular house, I had said: "That's the house where I was born."

"I thought everybody was born in hospitals," she said, in the innocence of her space age knowledge.

And it occurred to me that fewer and fewer people these days can point to a house as the scene of birth rather than a hospital. And so I went back one day to that street and parked the car and looked at the house in which I had been born on a bleak and wintery day—I am a Capricorn of course—on the third floor of an ancient building in another time and place.

One reason I returned was a song I'd heard on the radio, a marvelous and melancholy anthem called "Alone Again, Naturally," by Gilbert O'Sullivan, which has a verse that goes:

> In looking back over the years
> At whatever else appears
> I remember I cried when my father died
> Never wishing to hide
> The tears.
> And at 65 years old,
> My mother, God rest her soul,
> Couldn't understand
> Why the only man
> She had ever loved had been taken . . .

All those internal rhymes, an elegy to those loved, some of them lost. Anyway, I drove to the old neighborhood and sat in the car, motor running, radio playing, hoping of course that "Alone Again, Naturally" would emerge on the humid air, but there were two commercials instead, back to back and then the new Joan Baez song, which is fine but was not suitable to my mood at that moment. I looked at the old house and I thought of the people out of the past.

I thought of my grandfather, such a good man. He owned what was probably the last horse and team in town and would take his grandchildren for rides. It was a proud moment sitting beside him as he tugged the reins. The horse's name was Dick (it always reminds me of that old joke: We don't know the horse's name—the horse never told us—but we call him Dick) . . . anyway, we'd ride on the team, especially in the haying season with my grandfather crooning to his friend, Dick. My grandfather was a cheerful man who liked horses and cowboy pictures and grandchildren.

I sat across from his old house and saw the barn that is now a garage. The old cherry tree under which he sat smoking his pipe is gone. At one time the house was flanked by two empty lots—one was his pride and joy, a garden; the other, a place where the men played horseshoes on warm evenings. No garden now, only lawn. And a ranchhouse in the other empty lot. No more the sound of horseshoes clanging after supper.

More changes. Aluminum storm windows and a blacktop driveway. The old shingles covered with asbestos siding. A fancy mailbox, wrought iron. And somehow, an absence of trees. I remembered climbing trees, grabbing apples and pears, and swinging the limbs, like Tarzan. I was a boy and my grandfather watched me with loving eyes—is there a purer love than that of a grandfather?—and I felt esteemed and safe.

I sat there on one of the hottest afternoons of the year and the radio now was playing a sentimental thing—I didn't get the title and couldn't understand all the lyrics—but it was sweet and tender. And I let myself ride on the waves of sentiment, thinking of spent days and lost evenings and people gone forever and remembering Ogden Nash's poem on the middle years:

> When I look back on bygone days
> I think how evening follows morn,
> So many I loved were not yet dead,
> So many I love were not yet born.

The kid said: "Hey, mister, your gas tank's leaking."

He was standing with his bicycle at the front of the car.

It wasn't the gas tank. It was the radiator, water splashing on the street, running in the gutter. I know next to nothing about cars but knew something was wrong. And figured I had better make a fast drive to the nearest garage.

Thus the mood was gone, the spell broken, the enchantment ended, the sweet remembering vanished. And maybe it's just as well. The past is no place to live and we should only make short visits to it.

And maybe Thomas Wolfe was right, after all, about not going home again.

That's what I thought as I drove to the garage where the mechanic on duty told me the bad news.

July 18, 1972

The Observer

Those Who Don't Make Headlines

I REALLY DIDN'T KNOW HIM VERY WELL. WE USED TO RUN INTO EACH OTHER once a week or so at a neighborhood drugstore and talk awhile. He lived near the store and it was his evening ritual to stroll to the place and buy a six-pack of beer, maybe, or some cigarettes. Then he'd stand around and chat with people who dropped in. He was a small man with a warm, friendly smile.

At first we'd only nod, and later on we began to strike up conversations. He had four or five grandchildren and liked to talk about them. He worked in a plastics factory and he looked forward to his retirement in a few years. He had plans to travel, perhaps go to Florida in the wintertime. Mostly he asked questions. He was intrigued by writers. He'd tap his temple and ponder the mystery of getting something out of your head and putting it down on paper. And having people pay for it.

He'd want to know, for instance, how many words there were in a short story or a novel like *Gone with the Wind* and this would start discussions and I'd find myself sounding off about writing and probably talking too much, but he always seemed to listen intently.

"I've always worked with my hands," he said, "with things I could see." But when he talked about his work there was pride in his voice. He talked about how a man paces himself through the day and outwits the time studies to get a better money rate for the job. He remembered the Depression and he'd say: "It's good to work and then relax in the evening with a glass of beer or two."

Sometimes we talked about the events of the day or the Red Sox and Bruins in season. On cold nights we'd stand near the oil stove, shivering when the door opened to admit a blast of frigid air. In the summer we'd linger on the corner as dusk gathered and the kids were called into the houses. The older teenagers would go screeching by in their cars, squealing their tires, and we'd talk about how it is to be young.

This went on for a year or two and then one evening I opened the newspaper and learned that he had died. A brief illness. Survivors: a wife, three sons, and a daughter. Five grandchildren. Calling hours, two to four and seven to nine. I had only seen him a week before and he'd been fine, lively as usual. I stared at the page until the letters blurred. And I felt a dim sort of anger.

I have always avoided funeral homes whenever possible because I prefer to remember people as they were, pulsing with life. Who doesn't, of course? Anyway, I showered and shaved and dressed up and drove to the funeral home that night. I sat in the car, asking myself what I was doing there. I could have been doing a dozen other things. I didn't know his wife or his family or his friends. But I got out of the car and crossed the street.

The familiar smell of the flowers assailed me as I opened the door and stepped inside. His name was posted on a kind of bulletin board with an arrow pointing to the proper room. I signed my name in the register and then stood there awhile, getting adjusted. I saw a cluster of people near the coffin. Probably a delegation from a lodge or the union. And then I saw, unmistakably, his wife and children.

She was dressed in black, as you'd expect, and was small and dainty. Even at that distance, I could see her weariness and her eyes like raw onions from too little sleep, and too much weeping. A young man stood beside her, his arm protectively around her shoulder. Two other fellows stood there, and a girl, white-faced but with chin on the rise. Three sons and a daughter. They shook hands with people and brushed cheeks and accepted condolences.

Finally I made my way to the coffin. Knelt and prayed but the words were hollow echoes. I didn't look at him. I thought: I'll really pray for him sometime but not now, not now. And then I stood up and turned to face the family.

His wife—widow—regarded me with polite puzzlement. "I'm sorry," I said, her hand in mine. "You don't know me. But I knew your husband. We used to talk. He was a good man." I have quoted those words but I'm not sure if those were the exact words I used. I think he'd have been interested in that: the problem of a writer— should you paraphrase or put it down exactly?

She looked at me blankly, numbly, and introduced me to her children, whose names I didn't catch. I felt like an intruder and I went and sat down in one of those terrible folding chairs that you encounter only in funeral homes or at beano parties.

People came and went and I sat there alone, my tie knotted too tight, wishing I hadn't given up smoking so that I could escape to the smoking room. I thought of the man who had stood with me on the corner near the drugstore, and how quietly we arrive and depart. And how a man can be born and later die without disturbing the universe, never making headlines and his death announced in eight-point type.

I thought of all the men, good men, who are born and who marry and bring children into the world. They work and make love and have good times and bad times and they love their wives and children without making a fuss about it all and then they die. I thought of my own father, who came and went and gave me life. The earth should stop turning for a while or lightning should split the sky when a good man dies. But nothing happens.

I sat there awhile among all those people I didn't know and then drove to the drugstore and bought a six-pack of beer and went home.

October 31, 1972

Beauty That Lingers

THEY WERE A LOVELY SIGHT TO BEHOLD, A CLUSTER OF LADIES OF A CERTAIN age, the age of blue hair and handbags and hats with flowers on them. They were walking down Fourth Street in Leominster one day last week, six or seven of them in the group. Apparently they had attended a meeting of the Golden Age Club or the Senior Citizens or something. Or maybe they had just gathered for an afternoon at someone's house for cards and coffee and were now going home.

They walked daintily, small, tentative steps, and one of them was doing all the talking. I was parked at the curb and watched them go by. They were listening intently to the talker—and the story must have been amusing because they were smiling and obviously enjoying themselves.

It was pleasant seeing them, no longer young but stylishly dressed, their children grown up now and probably their grandchildren visiting on Sundays and holidays.

I drove away after a while and didn't give them much more thought, until the next afternoon, when I was driving on Summer Street in Fitchburg. The day was one of those rare springlike days we've had this month, beautiful, the sun dazzling, the air warm and luxurious.

School was over at St. Bernard's and the fellows and girls were streaming out of Harvard Street. And that's when I saw them: a group of girls, high schoolers, walking along together, five or six of them.

They wore slacks, some were flared; and because the day was mild, their coats were open, revealing a rainbow of colors—sweaters and blouses. They walked in a small cluster in that slow after-school attitude when the day is lovely and who wants to go home and do homework or housework?

As I drove past them I made the connection between these young and sweet girls and the women I had seen the day before. For a moment the years were bridged—and I thought of how you can't stop time, how relentless it is, and how these girls of today will someday take that languid leap into age.

Conversely, it seemed as if those older women I had seen the day before were now suddenly before me in all the freshness of youth.

And instead of feeling sad at the thought of time passing and taking toll, stealing away so much of what we are, I had a sense of the continuity of life, the stages through which we pass, and how each stage has its own sweetness if someone cares enough to seek the sweetness instead of the bitterness.

There's a poem that has a kind of terrible beauty, "Blue Girls" by John Crowe Ransom, and I was always struck by the sad truth of the poem. Now I wonder if it is really true or not. The poem:

> Twirling your blue skirts, traveling the sward
> Under the towers of your seminary
> Go listen to your teachers old and contrary
> Without believing a word.
>
> Tie the white fillets then about your lustrous hair
> And think no more of what will come to pass
> Than bluebirds that go walking on the grass
> And chattering in the air.
>
> Practice your beauty, blue girls, before it fail;
> And I will cry with my loud lips and publish

Beauty which all our power shall never establish
It is so frail.

For I could tell you a story which is true:
I know a lady with a terrible tongue,
Blear eyes fallen from blue,
All her perfections tarnished—and yet it is not long
Since she was lovelier than any of you.

I have been drawn relentlessly to this poem across the years, and often when I've seen sweet young things I've thought of how finally beauty fails, how vulnerable beauty is. And it was always a sad thing.

But now I wonder, I wonder. I'm not sure if I'm saying this right or not, but there's another kind of beauty that remains and the poet wasn't talking about this other kind of beauty—the beauty of having endured and survived, of having known laughter and tears, and love found and lost, perhaps. I won't go into a lot of fancy description, because it's all been said before—how age has its own beauty despite the sadness of spent years—but it all came back to me in those two recent encounters.

So, practice your beauty, blue girls, but it doesn't necessarily have to vanish. The beautiful and the true remain forever, no matter what the poet says. I know. I saw it on Fourth Street in Leominster one afternoon last week.

February 28, 1974

The Sound of Glass Breaking

THE MOMENT WAS BEAUTIFUL. IT WAS A SATURDAY NIGHT TESTIMONIAL AT King's Corner Restaurant and they were dancing to the music of the Tony Conte group. The strains of "Sweet Caroline," the Neil Diamond thing, filled the air and it would help if you knew the song because it is absolutely marvelous.

And when I hurt,
Hurting runs off my shoulder,
How can I hurt when loving you?

Then:

> Sweet Caroline,
> Good times never seemed so good . . .

Anyway, anyway. The musicians kept repeating those four notes, Sweet Caroline, and the couples were rollicking and everyone was caught up in the sweet frenzy of the moment.

I sat at the table, a glass of beer in front of me, watching the people dancing. It was one of those moments when I wished I still smoked. Ah, well. I was enjoying myself because it was a fine evening with people I love and close friends and, of course, a testimonial always means an imminent marriage.

As I looked toward the doorway a movement caught my eye. A fellow and girl had been passing by, having evidently left the bar on the other side of the place. Hearing the music, they peeked in. They were in their mid-twenties, a nice-looking couple, and their faces were glowing.

Suddenly, seized by the music, that irresistible "Sweet Caroline" and Tony Conte shouting "That'sa nice," they started to dance right inside the doorway. The fellow held her close, they were cheek to cheek, and they whirled and floated and spun. And everyone else was spinning and whirling, too. It was a glorious moment.

The girl looked up into the eyes of the fellow, as if to confirm his presence, and then nestled in his arms again. Then the music stopped. There was that pause, when people exhaled luxuriously, the beat still echoing in the air, and there was the waiting for the next song to begin, because you don't ever want the music to end.

The young couple stood there, hesitantly, wondering what to do, and maybe feeling a bit embarrassed for intruding. Then the girl began to tug the fellow toward the door. He was reluctant and made a sweep of his hand, as if to say, They won't mind, let's dance again. But she stood at the doorway, looking at him, with a gentle appeal in her eyes. The fellow gave a quick backward glance at the musicians and then he went to her and took her arm and they left.

I said to myself, He loves her more than the sound of breaking glass.

I thought about breaking glass at that moment because the young couple reminded me of one of the most beautiful and heart-wrenching stories ever written, a thing called "Fifty Missions," by Joseph

Dever. It was written during World War II and won a short-story contest sponsored by *Yank* magazine.

It's the story of a young flier who had completed an incredible fifty missions over Europe and he's home now, back in Boston and going to see his girl, whose name used to be Jane and who is now a nun out in Roxbury.

In the old days, before the war, they worked in a playground and they loved each other and would kiss when the kids weren't looking, and they planned their lives together and wondered what their children would look like.

Then the war came and Jay, the fellow, became a gunner.

Now Jay is back and he's in a seventh-floor room of a Boston hotel and he looks out the window and sees only the white face of a nun.

Glancing out, he sees familiar places and he remembers . . .

"The Copley Plaza is over that way. And on the other side of it, about four stories high and facing Copley Square and the Boston Public Library, there is a little marble balcony. The night of my college senior prom I threw highball glasses into the square. I liked to hear the tinkling clatter of the glass against the cobbles, and I wanted to do it again and again.

" 'Jay, come inside' was all Jane had said.

"I went inside; I loved her greatly, more than even the sound of breaking glass, and I always did what she said."

It's a sad story and a beautiful one at the same time, and it tells of an impossible love and then of a greater love. Jay visits her in the cloister and they talk and touch hands, and when he begins to ache for her in the old way, he knows it's time to go.

They kneel in the chapel and Jay tells God he's sorry for not wanting to come back from fifty missions. And then he walks out of the chapel and into the street.

That's all there is, a brief encounter, the ache of longing, and—I don't know, maybe it's corny and sentimental, although the language is terse and the emotion wells between the lines.

Anyway, I've always remembered those words about the sound of breaking glass.

The thing is that love reveals itself in small ways like that. I mean, you can make big heroic gestures and buy her flowers every once in a while or remember birthdays and anniversaries and go wild with a shopping list at Christmas, but it's the little things that make up love.

It's loving someone more than your pleasure of the moment, more than the sound of glass breaking.

I have been wanting to write about "Fifty Missions" for a long time and I thought of the story again the other night when I saw that young couple at King's Corner Restaurant. They were so radiant and so obviously in love and he wanted to stay and dance and she wanted to go—and he went with her, because he loved her more than one more dance, one more song. It still happens that way and it makes you feel good.

May 23, 1973

And That's the Way It Goes . . .

THE REASON I CAN SEE SO MUCH OF WHAT'S GOING ON DOWN ON THE STREET four stories below as I sit here at the typewriter is that the window is very low and it's possible to look up and watch the comings and goings.

There is so much happening down on the street, although it's not always apparent at first glance. Small vignettes take place and they develop before your eyes and raise questions that are never answered, or tell stories whose conclusions you never see. But sometimes, an entire drama develops and you see not only the tip of the iceberg but the cold, lonely depths below.

Take the other day. Standing in the doorway of a vacant store—there's something about a vacant store that attracts people, who find it a place to pause and linger—anyway, standing there late one wintry morning were two men, a tall guy with blond hair whose hands gestured eloquently as he spoke and a smaller, chunkier guy who was shriveled in the cold and who kept his hands in his pants pockets most of the time.

The tall guy wore a raincoat—it looked wrinkled and slept-in. The other wore a dark jacket, buttoned to the neck. They were in their mid-thirties probably. The tall one did most of the talking while the other looked morosely out at the street, his chin at half-mast.

People passed them by and they didn't pay any attention as they huddled in the doorway, bracing themselves against the cold. I had writing to do and glanced at them once in a while and then turned back to my work.

Once, when I looked up, I saw that they had faded into the depths of the doorway. The small guy took a pint bottle—it looked like a pint from that distance—and handed it to his companion. The tall one threw back his head and gulped the booze. His body shuddered at the jolt of the drink. He handed the bottle back and the small guy took a long drink. It must have been his bottle because his drink was longer.

Then the bottle disappeared under his jacket and his hands went back into his pockets again, and they walked back to the mouth of the doorway and looked out at the street once more.

The tall guy was still doing most of the talking. He must have been telling a long story and he was a nonstop talker. The smaller guy was beginning to respond. Instead of staring bleakly into the street, he began to look up and make a comment or two of his own. Then, they glanced around, up and down the sidewalk, and faded into the doorway again. The ritual took place once more-the gulp, the swift shudder, the exchange of the bottle, and the quick tucking of the booze under the jacket.

This went on for a while, and now the tall guy was quieter, looking across the Upper Common island. The small guy began to talk more and he began to notice the people passing by.

He didn't seem so tense or morose. He still kept one hand in his pocket—from the awkward position of his arm, I figured his arm was safeguarding the bottle. With the other hand free, he gestured once in a while. He was looser suddenly and more at ease.

Three or four pretty girls went by—it was the noon hour now and some of the office girls were going to lunch—anyway, he'd say something to them. I couldn't hear what he was saying, of course, but it couldn't have been anything terrible, because they didn't seem offended. Some of them didn't even pay any attention to what he was saying and others glanced quickly at him and away again, almost as if they had looked up expecting to see someone, and saw no one.

The tall fellow was leaning against one of the window supports now, kind of quiet, not noticing the passersby, shriveled in his raincoat. He lit a cigarette and puffed furiously. He offered a cigarette to the smaller guy but it was refused. The smaller guy was having too

much fun. He was getting a kick out of talking to the people going by
—not only the girls but teenagers and old people. Maybe he was
saying "Hi" or maybe "Happy New Year."

The two guys drew back into the recesses of the doorway once
more, glanced around surreptitiously, and finished off the bottle. The
little guy had the final drink. He placed the bottle on the cement
floor of the doorway, propping it up carefully. Then a funny thing
happened. The taller guy picked up the bottle and tucked it inside his
raincoat. Why? Maybe he doesn't believe in leaving bottles around.
Maybe he hoped to squeeze out one last drop later.

They returned to the front of the doorway again, and now the
smaller guy was really loose. He wasn't out of control or anything.
And not drunk. But he had reached the marvelous stage of the glow.
His greetings were now happier and people smiled and sometimes
answered him, although nobody stopped. He was enjoying himself
immensely. The booze was working wonderfully inside of him. Never
mind the cold, never mind the need for the next bottle later. And the
tall guy was quiet. No more stories to tell. He didn't call out greetings. He stood there quietly, as if lost in thought, pondering—what?
The chances he might have missed? Or merely the empty bottle that
might still contain a drop or two?

Then they moved away from the doorway and began to walk toward the downtown section as if by some unspoken agreement. The
small guy wandered a bit on the sidewalk, holding his own all right,
but a little unsteady. He still called merry greetings to the people he
met. The tall guy shivered in the cold, making a comment now and
then but definitely not sailing, staring bleakly and morosely ahead. I
got up to watch them out of sight as they went—where? For another
bottle? Another fling at the strange thing that booze can do as it
works its mysterious way through the veins? Soon they were out of
sight and the doorway of the vacant store was empty again.

And that's the way life is sometimes on a winter morning in the
Upper Common of Fitchburg.

January 11, 1973

The Signs That Really Matter

THE SIGNS OF THE TIMES ARE EVERYWHERE AMONG US, VISIBLE OR NOT, AND they reflect the world we live in: signs on billboards and car bumpers that give us clues about what life is like in the dwindling decades of the twentieth century.

Take bumper stickers. Many people are addicted to them and they tell a story of travel and vacation. Ausable Chasm and Benson's Wild Animal Farm. Fine. And then there are the other bumper signs that go deeper, into the flesh, like slivers.

For instance, the other day I drove behind a car whose bumper proclaimed: "Warning—I Halt for Animals." My first reaction was: Beautiful. And my second reaction was: Wait a minute.

I mean, there's an implication in that sign that causes reflection. I'd never seen this particular sticker before and it made me pause because, although I always stop when there's an animal in danger from my car, I don't have a sign saying so.

I stop for children, too, and older people. Once I even halted to remove from the street a box that had evidently fallen from a truck. But it would be difficult to get all these things on a car bumper.

Now I'm not berating anyone who puts any kind of sign or sticker on a car bumper. What bothers me is that it's a symptom of the times and kind of worrisome.

Take, for example, the car sticker that says: Honk if you love Jesus. Why should I have to blow my horn to display evidence of any kind of love for anyone or anything? And why should anyone want me to?

We live in the kind of world where there is so much insecurity, where people seek such protection in the pack, in uniformity, that they always have to be reassured.

Hey, he's honking his horn at us. . . . He loves Jesus.

But I immediately think of the converse situation and I imagine people in that car also saying: *Hey, he didn't honk his horn at us. . . . He doesn't love Jesus.*

Which renders the sticker meaningless, doesn't it?

All these stickers exist, of course, because some entrepreneur correctly reads the apprehensions of the age and figures out how to make a quick profit. I imagine they are the same people who turn out the political campaign buttons and stickers.

The funny thing is that we also live in an age in which most people don't pay attention to signs. It seems to me there's always a fellow smoking a cigarette under the "No Smoking" sign. And there's always the car parked at the "No Parking" sign.

These people infuriate me. I mean, these signs are usually placed for a reason, and the reason is usually safety. The man smoking in the crowded theater or the cluttered department store threatens the safety of others. And the driver of the car in the "No Parking" space also threatens safety. Maybe the sign is there because the area is too narrow and the absence of parking allows a fire truck or an ambulance to pass more easily. I always wonder about the kind of people who smoke in "No Smoking" places and park in "No Parking" spaces. Who are they, anyway? Do they think the laws don't exist for them?

A while back, the fire department in our town was feuding with the mayor about a new work contract. The firefighters paraded in front of City Hall and the mayor's office, displaying signs that asked people to blow their horns if they supported the firemen.

The racket was deafening. Drivers waved to the picketers and blew the horns and there was an atmosphere of approval. But later, a fellow and I were talking about the situation. He said, sure, he'd blown his horn because he knew the firemen; some were his friends, and how could he *not* blow the horn?

And he added: "But I also know the mayor, and if he'd been standing there I'd have blown my horn for him, too."

I suppose I shouldn't be bothered by things like this, but I am. Most of the time I search in vain for signs that have wit and humor, but the only funny one I've seen recently was scrawled in the dust clinging to the side of a dirty truck:

"Please wash me."

Anyway, I guess the point that I'm trying to make is that the signs are all around us and they cancel each other out in the end. Meanwhile, the signs that really matter are the ones that people seldom see —the small signals of distress from people in need of help.

These are the S.O.S. signals of the spirit, people crying out desperately but silently for assistance and aid, for tea and sympathy, compassion. And love.

There's the telephone call that goes on too long simply because the person at the other end of the line can't bear the thought of the silent rooms after hanging up.

There's the fellow who corners you in the hallway with the long, involved story without much of a point but who needs to be reassured that he's just fine, he's well liked, he's clever, he's needed.

There's the girl in the dress that's all wrong for her, but who is trying to break the deadly and monotonous routine of her days and nights.

All the distress signals . . . people who are not sighing but crying, not dangling but strangling, not holding up but holding on, not asking but pleading. . . .

These are the signs that count. And sadly enough these are the signs that so many of us fail to see because you don't find them on bumper stickers. Or do you, after all?

January 1974

Despite the Fun and the Frolic

DESPITE THE FUN AND THE FROLIC AND THE FANTASY, AN AMUSEMENT PARK IS filled with drama, not the huge dramas of life and death perhaps, but the small wrenchings of soul and spirit. A park is peopled with poignance, simply because there is so much at stake in many ways. The games of chance exist to challenge the player—and often the challenge both exalts and assaults the participant. For instance:

He came along in the crowd with his wife and two sons, the boys about eight and ten years old. He was a big man but gentle somehow in his swagger, the kind of fellow who wears a long-sleeved shirt, sleeves rolled up, which bulges the muscles of his arms. The sun sparkled on the family as they strolled the midway. I had paused to rest in the shade of a young maple, my small daughter docile beside me, awed by the sights and sounds.

They stopped in front of the "Sock It to Me" game, which is simply a new name for an ancient contest: lift the mallet high above the head, slam it down with purpose and determination in an effort to lift the small weight to the top of the pole. If successful, the player hears the sweet music of the bell sounding. Twenty-five cents for three chances. For a moment there he hesitated and raised his eyes to the top of the pole where the word "Superman" was printed. "Hey, Dad, I'll bet you could ring the bell anytime," one of the boys called.

It looked so easy, and the father was so majestic in his manhood, and the day was so lovely, a day when nothing could go wrong. He shrugged modestly and turned away, but the other boy set up a racket of pleas. "Come on, Dad, Aw, come on." The father looked at his wife and she smiled, quiet in her pride, and lifted her shoulders, the wifely gesture which means: Whatever you say, dear. What the hell, his manner replied. And he reached into his pocket for a quarter and stepped into the enclosure where the mallet waited.

A small crowd often gathers when someone accepts the challenge of the bell. I could hear the clackety-clack of the roller coaster, which is like no other sound in the world. Music was pumped into the air by the merry-go-round. The father lifted the mallet high and braced himself. The boys fell silent. And I didn't feel like watching suddenly. He had nothing to win, really. And I was afraid of what would happen.

The mallet struck and the sound echoed. The small weight soared upward. For that one flashing moment, it seemed certain to hit the bell, but it reached 1800 ("A Bit More") and fell back toward the bottom. The father was astonished. His aim had been so accurate and his strength had never been doubted. Without a pause—perhaps because he didn't want to face his family at the moment—he struck again. No bell. And then again. An emptiness in the air.

"Let's go, hon," I said, tugging the child's hand, but she was cool in the tree's shade and absorbed in watching some children skirmishing near the merry-go-round entrance. I didn't want to watch the painful scene any longer. Why must we always be witnesses to each other's defeats? And yet I didn't go. I looked at the father and saw the embarrassment and frustration in his eyes. He shook his head and reached into his pocket again. His manner said: There must be some mistake here, something wrong. The bell is supposed to ring. He somehow managed not to look in anybody's eyes.

He tried six more times—another fifty cents—and his efforts all were wasted. In fact, the longer he tried, the less effective the results. Once, the weight ascended to 1600 ("Aw, C'mon") and once it only reached 800 ("Weak Arm"). His wife looked around the crowd, with the smile that is not a smile at all. The lips smile but it is somehow horrible. After the first few attempts, the boys managed to begin scuffling with each other, although their eyes kept sliding toward their father.

Finally he raised his big shoulders in surrender. In front of his wife and sons and the small crowd, he exhaled slowly and stepped out of the enclosure, shaking his head. The boys were quiet, solemn. The wife kept looking around, as if saying to people: You know men, they're just overgrown boys really. The father still didn't meet anybody's eyes. I looked away. The sun continued to shine but its brilliance was diluted. I told myself: It's only a game, for crying out loud.

The family headed my way. As they passed, I heard the wife say: "Listen, it's a knack. It's got nothing to do with being strong. You hit the thing beautiful, beautiful." She pronounced it beau-tee-full. He looked at her sheepishly. "Beautiful," she said again. And he took her hand. The boys were scuffling again and then began calling out to go on the Dodgem. I watched him and her strolling hand in hand. And I thought: How precious are these women who love their men so much they turn small tragedies into triumphs. Ringing a bell has nothing to do, really, with what a man is, and what he knows he is to his wife and children.

June 4, 1970

Return to the Bridge

I VISIT THE BRIDGE AT CONCORD EVERY ONCE IN A WHILE.

And whenever I do, my soul is nourished and my spirit is restored.

I've made pilgrimages there in all the seasons of the year, in gloom and sunshine. One May morning, the rain slanted down and the bridge was hushed and still, deserted except for us. A certain child picked damp flowers by the side of the dirt road and brought them to her mother, with pride and love. And that was a beautiful visit even though we all got soaked.

The bridge is always beautiful to visit even when it's crowded with visitors. Somehow, people visiting there seem to walk softly and talk in subdued tones. It's as if everyone is hearing echoes of that April morning when the Concord and Lexington farmers gathered to meet the foe at the rude bridge that arched the flood.

That's what the bridge does—it brings history alive. It's a living museum, vivid, immediate.

And that's why I went there this past weekend. I needed again to be reminded of the beauty and greatness of our land.

* * *

I had the blues last week. I had the blues because I was sick and tired of being lied to. And being let down. I was tired of being proven wrong. I mean, I have no emotional ties to Richard Nixon. I loved Harry Truman and was dazzled by the style and grace of Jack Kennedy. Nixon left me cold and yet he was the president. I love my country and the things the presidency stands for and I'm not ashamed to say it.

So we witnessed Nixon leaving in disgrace and we saw Gerald Ford deliver that simple but eloquent speech after being sworn in. And that made me feel a little better—the knowledge that the nation endures, we survive, we go on, we bind our wounds.

And I knew I would go to the bridge on Sunday. There are times when you want to go to church. But this was a time to drive to Concord.

The day was sunny, shimmering with green, and the child dashed into the bushes to gather whatever flowers were left.

This hasn't been her best summer. She has a missing front tooth which demolishes her smile and she's had chicken pox and the hives. She is getting taller and is at the awkward caterpillar stage waiting for the butterfly years. She is growing up, as all children must. The other day I was going downtown and asked if she wanted to come along. She always says yes. But that day she said she'd rather stay home. She was playing John Denver's "Annie's Song" on the phonograph. So I went downtown alone, feeling time slipping by too fast, too fast.

At the bridge on Sunday, we joined, oh, hundreds of people. Strolling along. Pausing on the bridge itself to watch the canoes passing below. At the house on the hill, we looked down at the terrain. A band of townspeople—men, women and children dressed in the Minuteman uniform—marched slowly on the dirt road to the ruffle of drums.

As always, there was this sublime sense of history. It was a time to pause and reflect on the passing years and how we ourselves are a part of history.

Beyond the bridge, I beckoned the child and she followed me as we climbed a hill, reaching a stone wall. The people walked below. I thought of the Minuteman who might have stood at this same spot on that far-off morning, having left a child at home, maybe.

"Come on," I said to the child. "Let's ambush them."

She loves games and drama, and she laughed with delight: The plan was this: We would creep up on the others with us, and surprise them as they came around the bend in the road. Hand in hand we crept down the hill. We hid behind some bushes and waited. And then we burst upon them, as if we were Minutemen. But they hardly seemed to know we were ambushing them. We did it too quietly, I guess, not wanting to disturb the peace of Concord. But the child knew, and I knew.

So we walked along the road, chatting, smiling sometimes at people passing by—that happens at the bridge: complete strangers smile at each other—and the child's hand was in mine. She carried straggling flowers in the other hand. We paused again on the bridge and looked at the sprawling pond, dappled with boats.

Time paused. She was still a child and this was my country, although both are always changing.

I felt good suddenly.

August 15, 1974

Ten Years Ago Today

I QUIT SMOKING TEN YEARS AGO TODAY.

And I'm still dying for a cigarette.

Of course, ten years ago I was dying of a cigarette. Not just one but many. Maybe a pack and a half a day.

The funny thing is that I could sometimes go for hours without a cigarette. But there were times when a cigarette was absolutely necessary. After a cup of coffee, for instance. Or at a party, when the cigarette was a valuable prop.

I mean, take a cocktail party where you encounter strangers or people with whom you've had only a nodding acquaintance. You could almost hide behind that cigarette, and the smoke that can become a veil. In an awkward moment or when you were gathering your thoughts for a remark that was supposed to be clever but seldom was, you could always stall by fumbling for a cigarette, lighting it up, and taking that first sweet inhalation.

But cigarettes were most important for me when I worked, when I sat at the typewriter, summoning words to be set down on paper. If a word eluded me or a thought was too vagrant to be pinned down, I'd pause and inhale the smoke. Somehow, that pause, that gesture, would bring forth the word, would capture the thought.

And I always figured that I could never give up smoking, because then I'd have to stop writing, the words simply wouldn't come.

The thing about smoking is that I loved it. I never grumbled about smoking, the way other people did. Oh, I coughed a lot and didn't have much appetite, but, hell, everybody seemed to be on a diet anyway. I burned holes in my clothes, and my thumb looked like a yellow thimble.

But I loved smoking and I didn't go around saying "I ought to give it up." And I didn't try a thousand times to stop. I loved the smoke curling caressingly in my lungs. I loved emerging from a movie, where I hadn't smoked for a couple of hours, and lighting one up—beautiful.

But even though I could forgo smoking for hours at a time, I'd plunge into panic if I found myself, say, at three in the morning, without a cigarette in the house. I'd search ashtrays for old butts, singeing my eyebrows with the flame of the match.

It was worth it, however, because smoking was such a pleasure.

But the time came when I realized that, for me, smoking was a pleasant kind of suicide. Now, I'm not a reformer and I've never gone around saying people shouldn't smoke. I let you do your thing and you let me do my thing. But I came to the point where I knew that I was one of the people cigarettes could kill.

The X rays told me. The twenty-four-hour-a-day coughing told me. The weight loss told me. Someone I loved, whose blood also ran in my veins, died of lung cancer. And I was convinced that cigarettes were slowly killing me. Maybe they weren't killing other people—but I felt they were my murderers.

I decided to stop smoking. I didn't want to fool myself by saying I'd cut down. And I didn't want to substitute a pipe. I simply quit. Cold. On a bright January afternoon ten years ago, I smoked my last Marlboro, put it out, and have never had another cigarette.

And I was so sad, so sad.

I won't go into all the withdrawal pangs, the daily longings, the half-agonies, the fumbling in my shirt pocket for the pack that was no longer there. Someone nearby would light a cigarette and I'd lean forward, trying to inhale some of the smoke.

The thought of never smoking again was harrowing—so I invented a game: I told myself that, any day now, they'd discover a safe cigarette and I could start smoking again. Funny thing, I still tell myself that.

It didn't take long for me to realize the benefits of not smoking. The cough cleared up in a few weeks. The weight loss was gained back. My appetite picked up, but food didn't taste any better. I remember dining at Locke-Ober's in Boston and remarking that the food tasted the same as when I was smoking. But food has never interested me that much, anyway.

The strange thing is that I was able to write without smoking. Oh, it was agony for a while, but the words and phrases, the similes and metaphors, came when they were summoned.

The most beautiful part of it all was that I had a sweet sense of life renewed, that I had taken a giant step in life. That I had turned away from suicide. If that sounds melodramatic, then let it be. Somebody else I loved, whose blood runs in my veins, died of lung cancer only a short while ago.

Our lives are made up of small pleasures—the big soaring moments come only occasionally. And these small pleasures, like smoking, make up the fabric of our days and evenings. But there is something sweeter than all the small pleasures, of course.

And yet, and yet.

It's ten years today that I gave up smoking and I'm happy I did. But there's a part of me that will be sad forever.

January 16, 1975

Poetry of Violence, and a Knockout

IN THE AFTERMATH OF HIS MENACE HE IS A GENTLE FIGURE AS HE APPEARS ON the show, his eyes a bit troubled and brooding at first, and then lighting up, an imp that lurks inside him suddenly leaping into view.

There have been rumors and reports of troubles in his declining years —illnesses and other plagues of the flesh and spirit—and the sadness of spent years clings to him like an aura. He is an aging hero, but a hero all the same, and when another championship battle looms he is sought out for statements and conjectures and predictions. And we listen to him because he matters to us. He was part of our halcyon days and thrilled millions of us once upon a lovely time. His name is Joe Louis.

Even those who don't enjoy the calculated violence that occurs in the squared circle called, for some reason, The Ring, are often beguiled by the events of "Fight Week"—those days which precede a championship bout. In the places where fight talk is important—the bars and the clubs and the lobbies—the arguments go back and forth. And the conversation returns inevitably to former times and other bouts. And there is almost always an argument about some date, some knockout, and somebody calls to the newspaper to settle the issue. That's part of Fight Week, whether the bar is on a Manhattan side street with sawdust on the floor or on Main Street in places like Fitchburg and Leominster.

And if the talk gets around to former times, then it must focus for a moment on Joe Louis. On that same show, Howard Cosell was a guest and sat beside the former champ. The talk got around, as it always must, to the two Louis-Schmeling fights. Cosell was asked to set the scene so that the viewers not familiar with the fights could have the background. In doing so, he quoted from a story written about the second Schmeling fight by Bob Considine. He could only repeat a few lines, of course, but for a moment there was poetry abroad in the night as Considine's words danced again in the memory.

Louis was at the height of his glory in those days of the thirties, swift and savage but curiously gallant. He was the kind of boxer who got married in the afternoon and then that night climbed into the ring with Max Baer and knocked him out in four searing rounds. And then, less than a year later, the terrible lightning struck. Louis, our Brown Bomber, our Golden Boy who had brought grace to a sport that was so often tarnished and tawdry. Suddenly Joe was knocked out in the twelfth round by Max Schmeling, the heavy-browed German who had been labeled by sportswriters as "The Condemned

Man" before the fight started, with Louis established as a solid, 10-to-1 favorite.

If we loved him in his glory, we also loved him in defeat, especially when Joe mumbled in his accent that echoed the Alabama of his birth. "He jes' whipped me, Ma," with no excuses and no accusations. He merely prepared his revenge and it was two years later, almost on the same date in June, that Louis again faced his opponent. Drama was rampant. Hitler sent Schmeling a telegram. Schmeling of the Super Race was supposed to prove Aryan supremacy before the world. The fight was held—and here is how Considine described that one incredible round in a dispatch over the wires of the International News Service on June 22, 1938:

> Listen to this, buddy, for it comes from a guy whose palms are still wet, whose throat is still dry, and whose jaw is still agape from the utter shock of watching Joe Louis knock out Max Schmeling.
>
> It was a shocking thing, that knockout—short, sharp, merciless, complete. Louis was like this:
>
> He was a big lean copper spring, tightened and retightened through weeks of training until he was one pregnant package of coiled venom.
>
> Schmeling hit that spring. He hit it with a whistling right-hand punch in the first minute of the fight—and the spring, tormented with tension, suddenly burst with one brazen spang of activity . . .

Here are selected sentences from the story:

> Louis caught him with a lethal little left hook that drove him [Schmeling] into the ropes so that his right arm was hooked over the top strand, like a drunk hanging to a fence.
>
> Louis—his nostrils like the mouth of a double-barreled shotgun—took a quiet lead and let him have both barrels.
>
> The white towel of surrender which Louis' handlers refused to use two years ago tonight came sailing into the ring in a soggy mess . . . The referee snatched it off the

floor and flung it backwards. It hit the ropes and hung
there, limp as Schmeling . . .

Of course, this isn't pretty writing—it is violent poetry, capturing
the terrible beauty of The Ring as probably no other fight story ever
did. Considine froze it for us—the action that people listened to in
Depression parlors, ears bent toward the old Emerson or Atwater
Kent and which others saw in the Saturday afternoon darkness of the
theater between Movietone News and the Pete Smith Specialty. Poetry doesn't always come in rhyme and verse. It can be movement and
sound—or the words clattering from the typewriter of a reporter at
ringside, capturing the sweet revenge of a fighter who, for the moment, was all of the boys in the world who also wanted to be cham-
pion of something.

March 9, 1971

The Governor Visits

HE STILL RIDES THE SUBWAY TO WORK EVERY DAY AND HE TAKES HIS COFFEE
with two (!) sugars—that exclamation point is suggested by the wry
look on his face as he says "Two"—and he still gets up every morning
about quarter to six, give or take a few minutes.

Michael Dukakis, Governor, 1976.

He strolled into the *Sentinel and Enterprise* newsroom the other
morning at 8:15 sharp—a terrible hour for a visiting politician. He
wore a suit whose color was a blend of green and khaki, a gleaming
white shirt with a subdued wine-colored tie, green socks, and wing-
tipped cordovans. His black hair was so neat it looked as if it had been
applied with a paintbrush.

He sipped his coffee from a styrofoam cup and ate a plain doughnut. He was relaxed and comfortable and obviously enjoying himself.
When he first arrived, he circulated in the newsroom, saying hello to
the reporters and editors and shaking hands. Hundreds of politicians
—senators, representatives, candidates—have done the same thing
here across the years and the ritual never varies. This pressing of the
flesh seems to renew them, confirming their identity or something.

His car was parked across the street at a parking meter. Modest car, blue. There have been times when politicians arrived in big black limousines, escorted by personal aides and the inevitable local politicians who always act like ushers at a wedding. That's not the Dukakis style. He was accompanied by only one aide—you need somebody to keep an eye on the clock and come in to say "Only five minutes more, Governor"—and Mike Kenney, a *Boston Globe* reporter. The aide did the driving.

Frankly, politics bore, as I have stated before in this space—but I am intrigued by politicians. I get a kick out of observing the way they handle themselves.

In a way, these visits are so similar that they could have been programmed by a computer. A couple of days before the visit, the governor's office phoned to say he'd be in the area on that particular day.

He'd like to drop in at 8:15. In the morning.

He'd have to leave at 8:45. Sharp.

"He's always punctual, right on time," the aide says. "And he's got to leave at quarter to nine. He's due at the mayor's office at 8:50."

The aide says that the visit will be strictly informal, no big issue to discuss.

He will be doing what they all must do, of course. Meeting people, making himself visible, exposing the man behind the headlines, and hoping people will like his style and remember that style when next they vote.

Although there was no publicity about the governor's visit to the office, word gets around. Or maybe it was coincidence that Chris Bicoules showed up a few minutes after the governor arrived.

Chris Bicoules is Greek.

And Michael Dukakis is Greek.

Chris happened to stroll by the door and the governor spotted him. He got quickly to his feet, shaking hands, saying something about Greeks meeting each other.

The meeting of the two men was warm, and casual, two old friends encountering each other. Chris towered over the governor, as he towers over most people.

"I'll see you afterward," Chris said.

Ellen DiGeronimo arrived and the governor was on his feet again. He embraced her—another warm greeting. He congratulated her for her recent victory: she was elected Democratic State Committee-woman in the primary election.

Ellen was armed with portfolio and papers. She is always armed with portfolios and papers—this is what makes her such a good politician. She is all business and all charm, all the time.

So the meeting went on.

The governor was questioned about issues and he handled them—even the tough ones—with ease.

His style is low-key.

He was asked a question about when he'd appoint a judge in Leominster and he thought for a minute and said that frankly he didn't know. He apologized for not having the answer.

This is refreshing in a politician—admitting that he doesn't know something. And apologizing. Most of them give some kind of answer, even if it's double-talk.

Actually the governor was very well informed and knowledgeable. He didn't duck any questions and he was optimistic about things without going overboard.

Sure enough, the aide who'd been lurking outside came in and said: "Five minutes more . . ."

And five minutes later, after another round of handshakes, the governor left.

8:49 A.M. Close enough to call it right on time.

March 17, 1976

Home

The Way Life Is: An Afternoon Visit

A TWO-AND-A-HALF-YEAR-OLD GIRL-CHILD HAS NO BUSINESS ROMPING IN A cemetery.

Her hair flies in the wind and her brown eyes sparkle. She pirouettes across the grass. But grass is different here: grass in front of a house is a carpet, grass in a cemetery is a cloak.

The child, whose name is Renée, sees only the wind-chased clouds above and the emerald of the lawn. The slab and stone of monuments are alien to her world. She has not yet learned to interpret the codes of tragedy.

We had stopped at the cemetery on impulse, while taking a ride on a hot day when she was restless at home.

As soon as I halt the car and open the door, she darts away. Free.

The afternoon is hot but a breeze comes up now and then. The breeze ripples an invisible wave across the grass blades and tousles the flowers planted here and there before the stone markers.

"Flowers, Daddy," she cries happily.

"But you mustn't pick them," I tell her.

She bends, daintily, the way girls are dainty at two and a half, and sniffs delicately, inhaling beauty.

Satisfied, she wheels and runs away again, through the grim aisles. Her laughter sprinkles the air with gaiety.

She exults in the freedom. There are no fences here. No gates. It's not like a street which your parents tell you not to cross because of the traffic. It's not like a store where she rides in a shopping cart.

She turns and waits for me, too timid to run too far, and I catch up to her.

I hold her hand as we walk, and I have to stoop a bit because she's so small. The streets of the cemetery are not tarred—they are made of small stones of various colors.

She is fascinated by stones and rocks and leaves. She picks up a handful of pebbles, elated at their colors.

She sees a carved angel and marvels at its grace and beauty.

She is too young for me to mention certain things.

I walk by the stone that marks the grave of my father, whom I loved so much. Nearby is the grave of my good friend Clarence. Further away are the resting places of my grandparents. On the other side of the cemetery is the small stone above the grave of my brother, who died when he was three. And all around, the echoes of friends I knew. So many.

She continues to run and strut.

I feel vulnerable and aware of the briefness of things. But she sees only the loveliness of the grass. She lifts her face, like an offering, to the breeze.

"Run, Daddy, run," she challenges.

I follow as she runs.

I am glad she sees only the beauty there and not the sadness.

I thought at first it was a mistake to take her there.

But as I see her frolic in her innocence, I realize she is part of my own immortality.

Clutching at comfort with this thought, I take her back to the car.

And as I leave the cemetery with my daughter on that warm afternoon, I don't know whether to smile or cry.

September 16, 1969

The Afternoon of a Reindeer

WHAT WE HAVE TO REALIZE, OF COURSE, IS THAT THEY HAVE LONELY, REST-less days, just as grown-ups do, and you can't simply dismiss them and say: Go and play, or read a book or something. They may be children but they, too, can be assaulted by the blues or that vague restlessness we all know on occasion. Oh, the sun is shining, and the television figures are dancing, and there's a lot of good stuff to eat in the house. But something's askew. It began earlier when she couldn't find her blanket. Her yellow blanket. At three and a half, that blanket is vital. Especially after she has announced that today she's not a little girl at all but a reindeer and her name is Cupid (after one of Santa's reindeers), and a reindeer in particular needs a blanket for protection against the winter chill.

I accept the fact of her being a reindeer. Sometimes she's a bird and sometimes she's a magician by the name of Lucy Starbright. Why not?

Hell, sometimes I'm a lion and sometimes a mouse. Or Bogart, on my best days. So the reindeer and I appreciate each other. Except at this particular moment when I have volunteered to baby-sit while others in the family go about various errands. I have blank pages to fill on the typewriter. Restless and bored, she hovers at my shoulder. She sighs. She counts to forty-nine, skipping all the nines, for some reason. Finally she says, "Reindeers like to play football." In her deep reindeer voice.

Now, if I were one of those exemplary parents, the kind you read about in slick magazines or view on television comedies, I would say brightly, "Fine," dropping everything. But there are two factors at work here. First of all, I'm writing under a deadline. Secondly, this football game is a killer, something I devised in a mad moment. We face each other a few paces apart. She extends her hands and catches the football when I toss it gently. But when she throws it back, I must juggle and gyrate and turn myself into an acrobat. Ridiculous. I happened to go into these gyrations when we first played and now she expects it all the time. She always laughs. Her laughter is so delightful that I play the fool to hear it. But I usually keep the game to a minimum. Exercise is not one of my strong points.

But we play. Actually, I'm glad to leave the typewriter: some days the words don't flow. We find the football and begin to toss it back and forth and her laughter gladdens the air. I jump and juggle and twist and she claps her hands. But enough of this madness. Now she wants a story. She thinks I am the greatest storyteller in the world and she cuddles while she listens. What man can resist such flattery and such caresses? I place a record on the stereo—Side 4 of George Harrison's "All Things Must Pass"—and proceed to tell her another chapter in the adventures of the mysterious Television-Turner-Onner. (It's not as bad as it sounds, really.)

I make it back to the typewriter. I replace George Harrison with an old 45. Joni Mitchell's "Big Yellow Taxi," by The Neighborhood. I let it repeat. It plays eleven times. She counts the times. Now she's hungry. And thirsty. Football again, Dad? No. Later: next month, next year. Soap operas on the television. Blank page in the typewriter. She sighs. I sigh. She brings me a book containing pictures to draw and puzzles—and those dot-to-dot numbers which, when completed, form a picture. "Okay, Lucy Starbright, let's try the dots," I say. "My name is Cupid and I'm a reindeer," she reminds me.

She's left-handed. The dots go up to 45. She has trouble finding some of the numbers and recognizes others. Concentrating fiercely, she connects the dots up to 19. The twenties bring her a little trouble. We try to figure out what picture is emerging. She pauses to rest. "What does 36 look like?" she asks. Then finds it. Now, she does something unexpected. She has switched the crayon to her right hand. Why? She shows me the left: her palm is damp with perspiration. She has been playing but also working hard. That moist palm: it kills me. Finally the dots are all linked. A rocking horse leaps on the page.

Expect no big climax here, no finale with a flourish. The others returned and it was time for *Sesame Street* anyway. I returned to the typewriter. The completed picture should have been symbolic. But that rocking horse doesn't do much for me. I think of that poor moist palm. More evidence that she is a person, growing up. I wonder what awaits her and think of the years ahead when an afternoon of playing with her won't be able to solve her problems. Now she thinks I am at least ten feet tall and the greatest man in the world and that nothing is impossible for me to do. I ponder the page. That dot-to-dot picture should have been a reindeer. After a while, I began to write this.

January 12, 1971

Beauty Flies Away

FRANKLY, THE MAN SELDOM CONSORTS WITH MOTHER NATURE. OH, HE'S aware of the miracles of sunrise and sunset and the mystery of the seasons and the marvelous balance of the planet in its precarious perch in the solar system. And although he pretends an indifference to the outdoor life, it's more of a family joke than anything else. He appreciates the perfume of lilac. And he is awestruck by the view from Wachusett or the first glimpse of Monadnock on the road to Baldwinville after leaving Route 2.

But he wasn't too impressed the other day when the woman brought home a couple of glass jars, with two caterpillars in one jar and a third caterpillar in the other. Both the child and the woman were excited by it all. An acquaintance of the woman, who gave her the caterpillars, assured her that the caterpillars would eventually curl into cocoons and later would emerge as butterflies.

The man squinted at the jars. Caterpillars aren't the most beautiful specimens in the kingdom of Mother Nature.

"See, they're eating the leaves," the child said.

True enough: there were chunks missing from the curling green leaves in the jars.

The caterpillars squirmed as they moved.

The child was so excited that he didn't say anything negative. He pretended to study the caterpillars but was actually waiting to get back to the Red Sox game on Channel 38.

The woman and the child decided to place the jars on a table in the screened-in room that juts out into the backyard under the benevolence of a kindly old maple tree. .

"Now we wait to see what happens," the woman said.

"Do you think they'll turn into butterflies?" the child asked.

"Let's hope so," the woman said.

Once in a while the man glanced into the jars as he passed. The leaves were almost eaten away. He never realized that caterpillars had such big appetites.

So began a daily ritual that culminated one day when the child, awed with excitement, announced that each caterpillar had transformed itself into a chrysalis. He and the woman accompanied the child to the jars, and sure enough, the caterpillars had vanished and in their place were three small green cocoons. But not cocoons, really. Each was a chrysalis, the child said.

"Chrysalis?" the man asked.

The child brought out the Golden Encyclopedia they'd bought a long time ago: one of those supermarket offerings, a volume a week for so many weeks. It was written for children but the man has always appreciated its simple clarity, especially when it comes to scientific matters.

Anyway, the encyclopedia explained all about butterflies and moths and the different stages and showed a drawing of a chrysalis—actually the pupa—and it was identical to the ones in the jars.

"Listen, maybe we'll see a butterfly after all," he said.

"That would be beautiful," the child said.

* * *

But the prospects appeared dim, after a few days. September turned chilly and the screened-in room was closed off from the rest of the house. The green of each chrysalis began to turn black and the child was afraid that this meant something was wrong. Days passed. A week, two weeks. The remaining leaves in the jar withered. The cocoons—the man never looked up the plural form of chrysalis and kept calling them cocoons—anyway, the cocoons were entirely black now and lifeless-appearing. Rain lashed the screens. Frost appeared one morning, winter's pale scout.

And then, last Thursday, the child arrived home from school and checked the room. Her voice was vibrant with excitement as she called: "The butterflies are here . . . they're here."

And sure enough. Two of the cocoons had turned into vivid monarchs—hectic orange and black with a latticework of white at wings' edges. Gently they were removed from the jars and placed on the floor. The wings of one butterfly fluttered tentatively.

"It's moving," the child said, awed.

The man had to admit to a certain amount of awe, himself. When the woman arrived home, she, too, shook her head at the marvel of it all.

Someone said that the butterflies ought to be assisted in their efforts at first flight. The child encouraged one butterfly to step into the palm of her hand. She carried it outdoors. She blew gently on its fragile wings. Suddenly, the butterfly flew, fluttering like an orange snowflake in the air, landing a few feet away. A moment later, it leaped into the air again. The second butterfly needed more coaxing but it eventually flew. Then it seemed content to remain on the grass.

The third butterfly emerged the next day, wings damp and closed. It was left undisturbed for a few hours—and then the child lofted it gently into the air with her breath. It flew briefly and then fluttered to earth.

"Aren't they beautiful?" the child said.

The next morning, the three butterflies were nowhere to be seen. The child searched the backyard futilely. The yard seemed lonely suddenly.

"I'm glad they were able to fly away," the child said. But she didn't sound too convincing. A kind of sadness softened her voice.

"That's where they belong—out there," the woman said. She didn't sound too convincing either.

The man thought about the butterflies, how they had emerged from the chrysalis and flown away. Like the child herself, emerging from the chrysalis of childhood, to fly on her own someday.

The man, the woman, and the child stood there for a while in the gathering dusk and then went inside the house.

September 23, 1975

"Love, The Fantom"

HE WAS A BIG GUY. HE WORE A LUMBERJACK SHIRT, AND A CAP THAT CAME down partway on his forehead. I saw him as I was leaving the downstairs business office after work. He was buying a newspaper in that dispensing machine they've set up.

As I came around the corner of the counter, I saw that he was accompanied by a little girl—oh, she couldn't have been more than two and a half or three. Her blond hair was tucked into her bonnet and her cheeks were McIntosh-red. Her eyes were lively and beautiful.

It was kind of crowded at the door. The door swings back near the dispenser and the three of us were caught in a brief traffic jam.

To make a bit of conversation, I nodded to the little girl and said to the big guy, obviously her father: "So you've got the boss with you." (A certain six-year-old of my acquaintance is delighted when I call her The Boss.)

He smiled and looked down fondly at the child. "No," he said, "she's my guardian."

I walked along behind them in front of the United Parish Church and the child was all excited about the orange F & L bus which had pulled up.

The father held her hand—and he's such a big guy, he had to stoop a bit to do it.

And I walked along thinking how our children are really our guardians, our watchers of the spirit. If there is a heaven—and there has to be—and if I get there—and I hope I do—I think my children will be my passport.

* * *

At the moment, this child of mine thinks that I'm the bravest and strongest and best man walking the face of the earth.

And for that reason I try to be the bravest and strongest and best man on earth.

And I'm glad that she doesn't see the times I fail, because I fail often.

There's something else about children. I know this is going to sound sentimental and kind of slushy, but I'm going to say it anyway.

Maybe the children are glimpses of heaven for us. How can you explain the utter delight a child brings to the world?

For instance, I came home the other afternoon, a migraine threatening the horizon of my brain and weariness heavy on my limbs. It had been one of those days—I was tired of headlines and deadlines. The weather had been bleak and grim.

I got home and went into the den.

And on my chair, I spotted a note:

Beware Of Danger
Love,
The Fantom

She's a good speller for six and a half, but I guess she didn't know about phantom. Anyway, I picked up the note and laughed and shook my head.

Now, I won't say that all my troubles fled the scene. I was still heading for the kitchen to have a couple of Alka-Seltzers and my gasoline gauge was still hovering on empty.

But suddenly there was a difference. And I knew she lurked somewhere in the house—the fantom—waiting to jump out and scare me.

The thing that I remember most of all, however, is how she wanted to scare her father and play the game and pretend to be a phantom, but she gave the whole thing away by the use of that word Love.

Like that big guy said, the children are our guardians. They guard us from worrying about ourselves too much, they guard us from losing our perspectives, they guard us from selfishness, from the emptiness of boredom, from the terror of loneliness.

Of course, they can get on your nerves, sometimes. Their favorite word is "again"—and there are times when five rounds of that Winnie-the-Pooh game she got for Christmas are enough. There are moments when you're not in the mood to read for the fortieth time her favorite story in her favorite book.

But there are the beautiful times when she's in the mood to crawl into the chair with you or when she can't resist adding "Love" to a playful note.

You go along, bungling a lot, and you try to be the kind of man your children think you are, and, like I said, you so often fail.

But maybe, just maybe, you get points somewhere for trying.

February 21, 1974

Ballerina, Turn Around

SHE HAS BEEN EIGHT YEARS OLD FOR TWENTY-TWO DAYS NOW—AND SHE IS very involved with arithmetic. For instance, she is four feet, three inches tall and she can jump four feet, two and a half inches from a standing position.

"Do you realize," she asks, "that with practice I'll be able to jump as far as I'm tall?"

From a running position she can jump five feet, ten inches. She also weighs 53½ pounds.

These days, she's always running up to someone in the house, announcing the latest statistic. This is very important to her because she is growing so fast and she now has a sense of her own growth and of taking her place in the world.

She can jog five minutes standing in the same spot. She admits she is weak in push-ups—she can only do three at a time. But she's practicing. She can do ninety jumping jacks. And when she swings in the backyard, she can go high enough so that her toes touch the lowest branch of the tree.

All these accomplishments. She can remember when she was so small that if she stretched out her arms, standing in the archway between the dining room and the living room, she couldn't reach the sides of the arch. Now she can.

And she can do Pepper 106 times with the jump rope.

She is, in fact, getting to be a real expert with the jump rope. It's beautiful to watch children skipping rope and singing those songs:

Not last night but the night before,
Twenty-four robbers came knocking at my door.
As I ran out *(she runs out of the rope)*
They ran in *(she runs back in)*
I hit them over the head with a rolling pin.
I asked them what they wanted
And this is what they said:
Ballerina, turn around *(she turns around)*
Ballerina, touch the ground *(she bends to touch the ground*
    with the tip of her finger)
Ballerina, show your shoe *(she hops on one foot)*
Ballerina, twenty-four skidoo *(she runs out of the rope)*.

So she goes through the days and evenings adding up the arithmetic that shows her progress. She has read *Harriet the Spy* five times and a book about teenagers (which she yearns to be, of course) called *The Real Me* no less than eleven times.

And I watch her and all this arithmetic and ponder how much math and arithmetic are a part of our lives. There's such order and logic and even beauty in this arithmetic, and yet such terror as well.

And by terror I mean the inexorableness of it all. Twenty-four hours in a day (like twenty-four robbers) and 365 days in a year—and the inevitability of passing time.

The child turns eight and someone else turns eighteen—and suddenly high school graduation arrives and we are faced with more arithmetic.

The girl who is eighteen wears the cap and the gown, and something catches in your throat when she places the tassel from one side of the cap to the other. She has suddenly turned a corner into a new arithmetic. Behind her lie thirteen years (counting kindergarten) of school, and four more years of college loom ahead. There was the arithmetic of all those report cards—the time she missed the honor roll by one point and, I guess, the time she might have made the honor roll by one point.

It wasn't too long ago, it seems, that she, too, skipped rope and rushed in to cite her latest activity. But at eighteen you don't. Eighteen is being a young woman, and that means a certain privacy and mystery in your life. And this is the natural order of things. At eight you give all your secrets away—because the joy is in the telling. At eighteen, however, you are your own person, not a reflection, and the secrets are things of the soul. At twelve, for instance, she kept a diary in which she wrote down what happened that day. At eighteen, the events are written in the heart.

Thus the constant arithmetic in all of its beauty and logic and order. And its sadness, too. At eight she skips rope in the backyard and sings a merry tune. At eighteen, she is skipping out of your life—and the song she sings is a song of farewell, even if no one thinks it is at the time.

June 5, 1975

The Child Who Came After the Others

"SHE'S A LOVELY CHILD," THE WOMAN SAID.

"Thank you," I replied.

We were watching Renée frolic near the fountain in the park, the park that is a green oasis in the concrete and brick of the downtown business area. In the inventive manner of nine-year-olds, she had fashioned a small raft of sticks and twigs and grass, and was watching the raft now as it pirouetted in the water. I was relaxing on the bench, basking in the benevolence of the sun, and the most important thing on my mind was pondering why park benches are always painted green. The woman, white-haired and motherly-looking, sat at the opposite end of the bench, watching with interest the people passing by.

After a while the woman said: "Your grandchild?" Renée was making a boat now, transforming a maple leaf into a small sail.

"No, my daughter," I replied.

Her mouth formed a small oval of embarrassment. "Oh, I'm so sorry," she said.

"Don't be," I said. "I'm not."

This kind of situation has occurred several times in recent years simply because there is quite a distance in age between Renée and me, and I am not as young as I used to be—but then, who is? The wrinkles that used to appear on my face only when I laughed have now taken up permanent residency there, and I keep telling myself that the gray at my temples makes me appear distinguished, despite what the mirror tells me every morning when I shave.

"A late baby," the woman said with an air of discovery.

Now, there was a time when encounters of this sort would have touched off certain reactions in me. First of all, that label: *a late baby*. True, Renée was born when our other children were well launched toward life—the oldest seventeen and the youngest ten—but I have always resisted the easy labels that people insist on using.

Yet, there might have been a kind of guilt involved in my emotions. For instance, when we dropped Renée off for her first day of kindergarten, I suddenly became aware of how young the other parents were as they led their children from car to classroom. I thought: These people look barely old enough to be married, to say nothing of bringing their kids to school. And then I realized that I was comparing them to myself. I remembered that I had been their age when our first daughter had started school. I looked down at Renée and thought: You are saddled with a couple of old-timers, sweetheart. And I felt bad for her, this child we had wanted so much—had we done her an injustice bringing her into the world when the bloom of youth had faded for us?

Renée never seemed to notice the difference in ages. Oh, she came home from school once or twice and said that some children had asked her how old her mother was. But her mother had prematurely gray hair to begin with, a family characteristic, so all the children in our family were accustomed to that particular question. Once at summer day camp, where I picked her up in the late afternoon every day, she got in the car and seemed slightly annoyed.

"What's the matter?" I asked.

"Those kids," she said, tossing her head toward a group of children also gathered to wait for their rides home. "They don't know anything. They wanted to know why my father never picks me up, why my grandfather always drives me home."

"Does that make you feel bad?" I asked.

She pondered the question a moment. "They're the ones who should feel bad," she said, finally. "They can't even tell the difference between a father and a grandfather."

"Listen," I said. "I am old enough to be your grandfather."

She shrugged, a magnificent shrug, and changed the subject.

The matter of age has been there all the time, of course, and it's really not easy to shrug off. Those two-in-the-morning feedings have an extra measure of sweet torture when the parents are in their forties and not their twenties. Visits to amusement parks are not always amusing because old bones find it hard to absorb the jabs and jostlings of the Fun House and the Crash Cars and the Whip Machine. I drew the line at the roller coaster, felt bad, and then remembered that I had never gone on the roller coaster with the other children anyway. It wasn't a matter of age, it was a matter of fear—roller coasters have always scared the daylights out of me.

Renée and I have spent a lot of time at the library, she exploring the children's section, tracking down books on horses and medicine and puppet-making, according to her latest interest, while I browsed the stacks or spent time in the reading room, perusing the newspapers and magazines. We frequently visit a playground about a mile away from our home, and I relax on a bench while she swings and merry-go-rounds.

"Maybe I should be more active with her," I told her mother. "Take her on hikes and things."

Her mother regarded me with amusement.

"It's a little late to be starting that now," she said. "I can't remember when you ever took the others on a hike. And they turned out all right."

One of the delights of my life has been watching our children with their mother. I have watched them in the kitchen as she cooked and baked, in the den while she knitted or mended or did whatever women do with needles. I have watched her planting the flower garden with them, putting seeds out for the birds, helping them with their piano lessons. Our son has always carried on a bantering conversation with his mother through the years. They have a teasing relationship, filled with wit and affection.

And I realize that age has not altered any of this. Renée invades my easy chair and sends the newspaper askew—so did our oldest daughter, Bobbie, in much the same manner. Of course, Bobbie never had to tiptoe quietly after dinner, while her father took a nap, as Renée has learned to do. On the other hand, we let Renée stay up a little longer in the evening—age has mellowed the strict discipline of earlier years, perhaps.

So the fact of age is always there and can't be ignored. But how often we ponder the richness this child has brought to us at this time of life. The others have grown and moved out of our orbit. The years pass too quickly and we cling to them. I think of that as I think of Renée, this child who came after the others. I also think of that woman on the park bench who described Renée as a late baby.

Renée wasn't late—she got here just in time.

April 1977

Trying to Convince My Heart

THE SAD THING ABOUT BEING A PARENT IS THAT IT LEAVES A LOT OF EMPTY places in your life. Your children are always going away. Oh, they come back, of course. But there are some lonesome stretches in the meantime. They begin going away from the moment they're born, I guess, and as they get older, the distances get greater.

The sadness is a strange thing because you want the children to be free, to scatter, to search out their destinies, to go wherever life takes them. You want them to gulp the good rich juices of life. You would never handcuff their dreams or aspirations. Go, go, you always say. And yet while you revel in their travelings and delight in their comings and goings, you can't help but feel a little sad sometimes.

It begins early, this process of departure. There's a time when home is the child's entire world and Dad is ten feet tall and the smartest and bravest man in the world. And Mom is the most beautiful and gentle and loving woman who ever lived.

Then the child's orbit widens. Other worlds and other heroes are discovered. A crush on a teacher, maybe. Or the girl in kindergarten. Everybody chuckles over that first infant crush and yet it's the first foreshadowing of other departures.

* * *

Summertime is a time for goings-away. The kids are off to camp. Or the mountains. Or the Cape. And there's a lot of excitement connected with the excursions. They send postcards or call at all hours and then they arrive home, sunburned, exhausted, all their clothes in need of washing and ironing; and the words spill out of them as they tell their adventures. And you live their vacations vicariously.

Ah, the coming home. She prowls the refrigerator while she tells what happened and then stops right in the middle of a sentence to make a phone call— "Hey, Joyce, I'm back, look, I'll call you again later, but I just wanted to let you know I'm back; it was wonderful"— and then picks up the thread of her story without missing a stitch. And it's nice sitting there listening to it all.

Parents finally get accustomed to the departures and arrivals, and it becomes part of the fabric of existence. You sleep better when all the kids are under your roof at night but you learn that life isn't like that, so you accept it.

You also figure that you've become expert at good-byes after all this time. You've seen them off to college, off for the entire summer—and there's nothing new about it anymore.

But suddenly there's an unexpected pang, catching you by surprise.

For instance, the other day I drove Chris, who is still going on seventeen, to the bus terminal. She was on her way to the Midwest for a week or so. She was excited and just a little bit nervous, the way it is when you're starting out on a long trip. It was a fine, clear August morning, a beautiful day to be going somewhere. Her suitcase was packed. She clutched her handbag.

I guess we were the first ones to arrive at the terminal, although there might have been others waiting inside. I pulled up in front of the place.

"I'll get your suitcase," I said.

"Oh, I can do it, Dad," she answered.

At that moment a car pulled up behind us. She looked back and discovered a friend of hers had arrived, another girl going on the same trip.

Things happened fast then. She grabbed the suitcase and somehow managed to peck my cheek, all at the same time. Her eyes were flashing with expectation and her smile was like a sunrise. And off she went, ready to meet her friends—others were arriving now—and it was a great moment: the whole adventure ahead, a glorious morning, sixteen years old. Boy.

Her excitement echoed in me and I pulled away. And then came a small unexpected pang. I almost drove around the block to catch a glimpse of her, to wave good-bye again—it had all happened so fast—and then I told myself to forget it, to go my way.

Look, I wasn't maudlin or anything. No huge wrench of desolation. It was a happy moment, really. And yet there was that small disturbing note, like someone striking a low key, passing the piano, and it echoes in the air.

Like the whisper of September in the midst of August.

Hey, I told myself, this is ridiculous. There's absolutely nothing to get lonesome about. I know, I know. But try to convince my heart.

August 23, 1973

Look Who's Writing a Letter to Santa Claus

DEAR SANTA:

I haven't written for a long time—ever since I was just a kid and asked for things that could fit into that bag slung over your shoulder.

It's not because I don't believe in you anymore—how could I have, over the years, convinced my children that you existed if I didn't believe in you myself? But I always figured Santa Claus was for children.

Then, a while back, Renée, who's the youngest, said: "Why don't grown-ups ever write to Santa, Dad?"

I said: "Good question. But what, for instance, would I do with a bag full of toys?"

And she said: "You don't have to ask for toys, do you?"

This was a revelation, something that often happens if you hang around with kids a lot.

So, Santa, I address this letter to you, although it occurs to me that I really don't want or need anything new. Just let me keep what I already have. For instance, the little things:

Let me continue to enjoy cotton candy at a carnival and hot dogs at a ball game and cheese and crackers as a midnight snack.

Let there always be a long, cold glass of beer at the end of the day's work and someone to pour it for me.

Don't let anybody take away my weakness for Henny Youngman jokes:

First man: "Any cops around here?"

Second man: "No."

First man: "Stick 'em up."

Or my shameless fondness for Nitty Gritties, which, to be effective, must be asked—and answered—at the dinner table:

Question: "What do you call a bunch of people at a big church fire?"

Answer: "A conflagration congregation, of course."

After which they refuse to pass me the salt and the pepper or anything else, for that matter.

Let me continue to cry at sad movies and be delighted by the corny ones, and let the good guys win at the end, once in a while.

Let there always be someone to say "Bless you!" when I sneeze.

Allow me to remain a night person so that I can settle down with a good mystery at one in the morning, which is the only time to read a good mystery.

Never let me grow tired of old records—Glenn Miller and Tommy Dorsey and Artie Shaw—and allow me always to respond to those great Beatles songs because my children and I bridged the generation gap when we found out everybody in the house loved them.

Continue to let me enjoy:

The thrill of getting into the line that moves at the bank.

"Coming Attractions" at the movies.

The light turning green as I approach the intersection.

The smile of a pretty girl on the street, although she has obviously mistaken me for someone else.

If I don't always have a clever remark at my beck and call, at least don't let me make a fool of myself too often.

But don't let me be afraid to risk absurdity once in a while.

Let the year bring new books by my favorite authors—Graham Greene and William Saroyan and Bernard Malamud. And let them discover an unpublished novel by Ernest Hemingway that turns out to be even better than *A Farewell to Arms*.

Let me continue to be beguiled by language, to remain enamored of such words as:

Dazzle.

Hustle.

Hasten.

And all the ember words—from September to remember.

And cellophane. (Pronounced slowly: cel-lo-phane.)

Don't let certain people grow up too fast, although they long to dash into the waiting years.

And detain the escape from my orbit of young Renée for a while, and let her continue to believe that I am ten feet tall and able to open any stuck drawer in the house, untie any knotted shoestring, and repair any broken toy.

Let me enjoy nostalgia, especially when the family gets together at times like Thanksgiving and Christmas and we reminisce about the olden days and the kids like to ask—with mischief in their eyes—if they had automobiles when I was a boy.

But let me cherish the present: today, tonight.

In fact, let time stop once in a while and allow the marvelous moments of here and now to linger until their full sweetness is tasted.

Let me practice my deceptions and continue to get away with them:

To appear strong when I'm really weak.

Brave when I'm scared to death.

Full of wisdom when I'm actually groping for the right thing to say.

Calm when earthquakes are going on inside me.

And please, dear Santa, let the years deal gently with all the people I love.

I don't really have to sign this—because you know who I am, don't you?

Just as I know who you really are.

December 1976

The Wrens Come and Go

I WASN'T GOING TO SAY ANYTHING ABOUT THE WRENS BECAUSE I DIDN'T WANT to spoil my image as the last of the great indoorsmen.

Give me the comfort of a screened-in porch while I view the comings and goings of Mother Nature's creatures. Let others risk the mosquitoes, bugs, and various other risks of entering the woods.

Actually, the woods behind the house are kind of inviting. They are fine for dogs to roam in and children to romp in, and I keep meaning to get out there but something always comes up.

What I like about the wrens is that I can observe them from a window or while sipping something cool on the porch. They've been coming every year now and have become part of the fabric of our existence.

Actually, I don't know an awful lot about birds. The backyard is full of them and I see them darting here and there, and their bird songs are lovely to hear. I bought Peterson's Field Guide to the birds and also the records that accompany the guide and spent a few days listening to the bird calls, and I kept getting hooked on certain calls. For instance, the call of the mourning dove. I played it the way you would a favorite record, and after the thousandth time I kept getting hints that the people around me were quietly going mad. Or that I was.

Anyway, the early morning call of the blue jays often awakens us, and during the day the sparrows and some unidentified birds zoom around the place. On the morning of one New Year's Day, a cardinal appeared, perched outside the window, and then flew away, like a spurt of blood from an artery.

Ah, but the wrens. The birdhouse is attached to the top of the clothesline and every springtime they appear. Two of them. Obviously lovers, looking for a place to set up housekeeping. You know they've arrived, because they sound like doorbells ringing. They dart around the backyard, in swift swoops, chattering all the time, and inevitably they discover the birdhouse.

Then the female of the couple settles in and the male begins to furnish the house, constantly coming and going, bringing small twigs mostly but other stuff, too.

*   *   *

Wrens are small—you could hold one in the palm of your hand. But that would be impossible, of course, because no wren would stand still long enough for that. There's probably not a more energetic or harder-working bird in the entire kingdom, always busy, always flying here and there, stopping only for brief intervals on a branch near the birdhouse, checking the presence of possible enemies, maybe.

All during the springtime we hear the sound of those small doorbells ringing and it's nice to hear. And then one morning a certain child wanders into the backyard and returns with the big news: The babies have been born. We go outside and cautiously approach the house, and sure enough, small peepings emanate from inside. Later, the father is out swinging in the trees like a small, feathered Tarzan announcing the births to the world.

His trips to the house are different now. His beak no longer contains twigs and such but food for the family. Worms and bugs. He makes a thousand trips a day, seldom stopping. He pokes his head out of the house, darts through the air, and returns a minute later, his beak full of food.

I like to sit there late in the afternoon, the house quiet and the backyard dozing in the sun. Forsythia has long ago come and gone, and the last of the lilac has bloomed by the dooryard. The busy chatter of the wrens and the small peepings make a pleasant sound track. The wrens are old friends now.

And then the inevitable happens.

Suddenly, one day there's a silence in the backyard, no more the doorbells ringing, no more the small peepings. We approach the birdhouse and can sense the vacancy inside. The wrens have gone. Without warning or announcement, without a final burst of song.

It always happens that way. Every year the wrens are there one day and suddenly gone the next. The child hopes that maybe they have just gone for the day, that we will hear them again later. But that never happens.

So the wrens have gone and the backyard seems empty in the summer heat. We know, and the child knows, that the wrens will return next year—I like to think of them as new generations of the same family, but that is ridiculous, of course—anyway, we know they will come back, but there's a loneliness in the backyard.

And the last of the great indoorsmen finds himself feeling sad about the departure of a family of birds, of all things.

June 25, 1976

Suddenly, Another Birthday

SHE'S BEEN GIVING ME PRESENTS FOR THE PAST WEEK OR SO AND THAT'S HOW I knew that my birthday was coming.

The thing is that she can't bear suspense. She can't wait for the next minute to arrive, say nothing of next week. And so she places a "present" on my chair, the kind of present you get from a five-and-a-half-year-old girl. It's wrapped in leftover Christmas paper and ribbons.

She tells me I can't open it until my birthday arrives. A minute later she relents and says that I can open it after dinner. Then she says: "You can open it right now."

This has been going on every day. The gifts are beautiful.

I have received a drawing of a daisy with a lot of O's that mean hugs and X's that mean kisses.

She has wrapped up and presented me with thirty-six cents in assorted change that fell out of my pocket and which she retrieved under my chair.

She also gave me one of her most precious possessions: a weary-looking teddy bear that's seen better days. I gave it back to her by suggesting that she take care of it for me. She was glad to do it.

And so the birthday arrives and suddenly a man doesn't know whether to be happy or sad about it. The years go by and each birthday brings changes, and after a while you are grateful for having survived, because you think of all the people who haven't.

Some birthdays are strictly routine. I think turning twenty-seven was routine, nothing memorable about it. Another routine birthday was nineteen and still another thirty-three.

What I mean is this: Some birthdays are more traumatic than others. Turning thirteen, for instance, and becoming a teenager. Arriving at twenty-one and going into a bar and ordering a drink without worrying about not having an ID card. Turning the corners: twenty-nine into thirty and supposedly not being trusted anymore by the kids. And thirty-nine into forty, leaving Jack Benny behind.

There are the birthdays that no one ever forgets. The birthday that occurred during the first tentative stages of falling in love. And the year my father died. My birthday arrived months after he died, but for some reason I thought of him all that day.

The trivial along with the tragic: the time I gave up smoking three days before the birthday and told myself it was only a temporary thing and I'd have a glass of beer with an accompanying cigarette when my birthday arrived. Well, the moment came and I poured the beer and took out a cigarette and didn't light it. I didn't feel heroic or anything. I felt terrible. That was eight years ago and I'm still dying for a cigarette.

Now this birthday was approaching and it looked as if it would be one of those nothing birthdays. Nothing memorable at all.

One year older, and a few years ago the matter of age might have bothered me. There were a couple of birthdays a while back when I realized I wasn't young anymore and there were certain things in life I would never accomplish, and it was kind of sad somehow. But the sadness passes and something else takes its place. You see your own kids growing up and going through the small agonies and ecstasies and all the rest of it. And although you have no regrets at all, you know you'd never want to be eighteen again or even twenty-one.

"Happy birthday." A new sweater. The after-shave lotion that is supposed to bring me sweet trouble. The books and records. The gift that was sent for and hasn't arrived yet—isn't there always one of those? The traditional card at the office that everyone gets on their birthdays.

You don't look a day older, someone always says. You check the newspaper for horoscopes and things like "If today is your birthday . . ." They never have anything too glamorous to say about Capricorn, and this year I figured I wouldn't bother looking, but I did. "Today's native has talent for managing money . . ." the astrologer says. Boy, have they got the wrong number. I even sign the wrong end on the backs of checks, for crying out loud.

But the birthday arrives and you realize, of course, that it is kind of special after all. It's the people who make it special, not yourself. How can you celebrate a birthday alone? Happy birthday, hon. Happy birthday, son. And those X's and O's. Beautiful.

January 18, 1973

My Mother's Hands

MY MOTHER'S HANDS ARE NOT BEAUTIFUL HANDS.

They have never fashioned Chopin on a baby grand or transferred a technicolored landscape to a canvas, or designed a dress that spurred adjectives in Paris and New York.

They are ordinary hands. The fingernails are not long, not pointed or cultured. Manicured nails only get in the way when there's washing or ironing to do.

The skin is a bit rough, maybe, and the lines are deeply grooved. If a fortune-teller scanned the lines of her palms, the past could be clearly seen: the Monday washes, the darning, the scrubbing.

Jewels don't adorn my mother's hands. A plain wedding band circles the third finger, left hand. The gold has never dulled. When she pulls her hands out of the suds of the dinner dishes, the ring gleams.

Nothing unusual in that. Except that for nearly three decades, the ring has never been removed. It's a symbol now: a pledge never broken.

As I look back through the years, her hands are what I remember most.

There was the time bad news struck the family like lightning. I was just a kid then. After everyone was asleep that night, I got up for a drink of water. There was a light burning somewhere. Stumbling into the kitchen, dazed by half sleep, I saw my mother in the old rocking chair by the window.

Her eyes were closed but she wasn't sleeping, because her lips moved silently.

Her hands were folded in her lap. Entwined in a rosary. The fingers moved from one bead to another.

She was still a young woman then, I could sense the strength in those thin long fingers.

And everything came out all right the next day.

My mother's hands are kitchen hands. The kitchen is the Grand Central Station of my parents' home.

She sets up the ironing board while the talk goes on. Or concocts hot cocoa in winter. Or her own mixture of grape juice, orange slices, and lemon flavoring on hot summer days.

The family problems get solved in the kitchen. There's serious conversation or light bantering, family stuff.

Try to get her to sit down or relax. She is busy everywhere, filling cups, pressing food on you, looking for something to do.

Home, through the years, has become this: the kitchen, the ivy hanging out of a highly polished brass container on the wall, my mother presiding.

You think of childhood and your thoughts stumble on a thousand pictures of your mother's hands.

The hands that untied the knotted shoestrings, buttoned the winter coat, tweaked the ear, wrote the notes when you were out of school those times.

The hands gave your sister her first permanent, wiped your nose with a handkerchief that smelled of lilac, combed down the cowlick.

And later the hands ironed the white shirt the night of the big date, found the cuff links that were always lost, straightened the tie.

The things those hands created: the forgotten Maybaskets, the letters in the leaping scrawl she wrote to my brother in Europe during the war, the meals.

Tomorrow is Mother's Day.

Those hands will set the table, cook a dinner that becomes a masterpiece under her guidance. Afterward, she'll open the gifts the family brings. And all of a sudden her hands will become fumbling.

She'll be embarrassed by it all. Mothers always are. She still blushes sometimes even at her age.

And to cover it all, she'll shoo everyone out of the kitchen in spite of the protests.

Her hands will become busy again. Straightening the place out, as she always says.

Her hands. Just ordinary kitchen hands.

May 12, 1951

Father of the Bride

THE FATHER OF THE BRIDE IS NOT SPENCER TRACY, THE ACTOR WHO PLAYED the role with such style and suavity in that old film comedy. In fact, he's not even a reasonable facsimile. He is just an ordinary-looking man who walks down the aisle—and he doesn't just give away a daughter but part of his life, as well.

But then, he's been giving her—and all his children—away since the moment of their birth.

For every hello, there's a good-bye.

The bride had said that she didn't want to walk down the aisle in solemn fashion, her face veiled, her eyes downcast.

So the bride and the father strolled toward the altar with smiles on their faces for all to see, giving small nods of recognition to relatives and friends.

At the last moment, the bridegroom approached to claim the girl who in a few moments would become his wife. The father kissed the girl on the cheek—a hurried last-minute unplanned kiss. Somehow it seemed inadequate, but it all happened so quickly that there wasn't time to think about it.

All he knew was that he had given her away.

How many times had he given her away, really?

That first day of school.

The first wild crush—when she worshiped someone from afar with such sweet longing.

The time she had approached in the twilight of a holiday and said: "There's really no Santa Claus, is there, Dad?" And a small part of her still wanting to believe. It's that small part that a father loves so much.

He had given her away a thousand times during the years, saying a thousand good-byes.

And she was saying good-bye at the same time—good-bye to the teddy bear, good-bye to pigtails, good-bye to childhood friends to whom deep secrets were whispered as the stereo played the Beatles.

All those good-byes were now gathered into a radiant farewell at the altar.

Funny thing. The father was not sad at this particular good-bye, not as he had been at others. He was invaded by a strange emotion that edged on happiness, that bordered on joy—but wasn't quite either.

It's as if language has missed a beat and failed to supply a word to describe the emotion that is poised between such sweet happiness and a hint of sorrow, the pause between arrival and departure, the fragile territory that lies between something ending and something beginning.

That was the emotion the father knew—and probably what all fathers and mothers know on a day like that.

A father plays many roles for his children.

There's a noise in the night and he goes downstairs to check, playing the part of the Protector of the Home even while his limbs tremble.

He plays the part of rescuer—the time she got caught in the tree. Or doctor: applying numberless Band-Aids to scratched or bruised arms and legs. Or counselor—trying to summon the wisdom that he does not possess to guide her at important moments of her life.

The father of the bride was once the sun around which she orbited.

And now he is only a pale satellite while she moves in another universe.

Once he could make her happy by promising her the world, because her world was small enough for him to encompass and a bright toy could make her dance with delight.

Now her world extends beyond his horizons—and it's not his to give her anymore.

Fathers of the bride are strange people.

They are not quite in the wedding party.

They remain on the fringes and try not to look too baffled at all the arrangements a wedding requires.

They shake their heads in amazement at all the lists, the details, the shopping trips, the arrangements, the comings and goings.

The house shimmers with excitement—and the doorbell rings all the time.

It's impossible to resist the excitement, the holiday feeling, and fathers are soon caught up in it all.

* * *

The father of the bride thinks now of all this as he watches her at the altar. He thinks of her as child and woman, as daughter and friend.

Later they dance together at the reception and he swings her wildly. They whirl to the music and teeter precariously, her gown a flare of ivory. As they spin, he thinks that possibly he is making a fool of himself. But he has never minded playing the clown for people he loves.

In the swirl of the day, in the music and the laughter, the poignancy is muted. Each drink is a toast to yesterday—each song a promise for tomorrow.

He never wants the music to stop.

And in his heart it never does.

March 25, 1975

When It's Time to Say Good-bye

THE STRANGE, ALMOST HEARTBREAKING THING OF ALL IS THAT AT THE FINAL moment of good-bye there is really little left to say. It's all been said before. Sometimes with words and sometimes without. With a gesture, maybe—a touch of the shoulder. Or a smile.

A man talks to his son in many ways through the years and most of the time it's everyday language. What's new? Don't stay out too late tonight. Do you need any extra money? The banalities that disguise the deeper things that seldom get said. The routine father-and-son exchanges. Hey, Dad, can I have the car tonight?

And sometimes the conversation is not so routine. The late-at-night talks that happen without warning, the sudden intimacies when the talk is about life and death, and the things a boy wishes to become and the things a man looks back upon. These are fragile moments on the edge of embarrassment because each seeks to preserve the other's privacy.

Then there are moments when the barriers come down altogether. The time the man stood in the hospital corridor waiting for the report from the doctor. The day the team lost by a lopsided score and the man saw the boy's shining spirit—the team had lost but had not been defeated. There were the times when the father stood in the football stadiums—shivering sometimes in the evenings under the lights—watching the boy in the uniform down on the field. My God, is that man down there my son, Peter, grown so fast so soon?

The years go by too fast and the boy is too soon a man and, finally, on a September evening on a college campus in a faraway state, there comes a time to say good-bye.

Saying good-bye to a son is far different from saying farewell to a daughter. You can hug or kiss a daughter. You can be sentimental with a daughter, although it may embarrass her. But she allows the sentiment. But how do you say good-bye to a son?

The first day at college is a busy time. Moving into the dorm. Where will the stereo go? The hustle and bustle. The strangers who will become classmates and, some of them, friends. The crowded corridors. The special programs for incoming freshmen and their parents. If the day is rainy, drenched with downpours, there's additional confusion.

And then, late in the evening, the campus is suddenly muted. The rain has halted but the trees still drip and the moisture bestows halos on the streetlights. At the last minute, the boy remembers something —his guitar is still in the car; it had been placed far back in the trunk, virtually tucked away from sight. And so the man and the boy walk across the quadrangle, through the footpaths, to the parking lot. The boy reaches in for the guitar.

And, suddenly, the moment for good-bye is there.

"You don't have to walk all the way back to the dorm, Dad," he says.

"All right."

"It's going to be great here," he says.

"We'll be leaving early tomorrow morning," the man says. He kicks at an invisible something on the blacktop.

The boy slings the guitar across his shoulder.

The two of them stand there, lit up for an instant in the flash of passing headlights.

That's when the man wonders: How do you say good-bye? You can touch his shoulder and shake his hand or embrace him, but hell, all of this seems both too little and too much. What do you say? Don't forget to write, especially to your mother. Make a joke, something about girls.

And that's when you realize that it's all been said, through all the years, and that all of life is a series of good-byes, for all of us. All the small good-byes that range from the first day at school to that first date, the first time away from home at camp, the first time a friend lets them down. Each of these is a kind of good-bye. Saying good-bye to childhood, to adolescence. All the good-byes that all of us say throughout our lives.

The father and son stood in the gathering dark, the evening having turned now to night.

Suddenly the son touched the father on the shoulder. A special touch that was both a light caress and a man-to-man contact. Their eyes held for a moment and they smiled at each other, shaking their heads in wonder as they stood there in the middle of the college campus. They had come a long way together, not merely in miles.

And then the boy—who was, of course, no longer a boy but a man, and had been for a long time—turned away. He walked a few feet, the guitar on his shoulder, and then turned again and waved.

The man waved back—suddenly happy.

He realized they had just said hello.

September 14, 1975

Father of the Groom

THE FATHER OF THE GROOM IS MUCH DIFFERENT FROM THE FATHER OF THE bride, although they may be the same person.

For one thing, the father of the bride finds himself caught in a kind of emotional no-man's-land. His head is aswirl at all the activity—shopping trips, invitations, flowers, a stream of oh's and ah's as the gifts begin to arrive, and an emotional pitch that becomes so high that it seems likely to shatter glasses on the shelf. The father of the bride watches all of this in bewilderment—although it is a sweet bewilderment—and he tries to look serene and wise and all-knowing as he sits on the sidelines.

The father of the bride is also gripped by poignancy. He thinks of his little girl—she will always be his little girl—going off with someone who was a complete stranger just a while ago. Can he trust this stranger with the girl who rocked on his knees all these years and smothered him with peanut butter kisses that tasted of Hershey chocolate on occasion?

The father of the groom isn't assailed by the same kind of emotions. And the pre-wedding atmosphere is different. The telephone doesn't ring constantly and there are no bevies of beauties sweeping into the house with the latest development on the wedding. All the action is taking place at the house of the bride. At the house of the groom life goes on as before. No emergencies about, say, the bridemaid's gown arriving in the wrong size.

But there are subtler emotions at work, just below the surface. The father finds himself looking differently at the groom these days. The groom had always simply been his son, a boy named Peter. Like all fathers, he took pride in the son of his flesh and spirit. He suspects that his own immortality begins in the life of his children.

He thinks of all the roles his son had played through the years— student, quarterback, bass guitarist in a group whose name he can't remember now—and memories run like a home movie through his mind. And like a home movie, the memories are sometimes helter-skelter and blurred and out of focus.

He remembers the time he went to the Saturday afternoon football field and saw his son calling quarterback signals. The man had never been the macho kind. But he felt like shouting to the crowd: "That's my son out there." His high school team that year was beaten game after game. But he never missed a practice and never whimpered. Losing by three touchdowns, the team still summoned gusto and spirit. The man never got around to telling his son that the team had had a real winning season that year, and it had nothing to do with scoreboards.

The father remembers the trips to the hospital emergency room. Somehow, that kind of thing doesn't happen so often with daughters. But a son does things like falling off a tree or getting his hand caught in the lawnmower. And the son also showed up late one night after being out with the boys, with the unmistakable smell of beer on his breath. So they had a Late-Night Talk.

The late-night talks were frequent, simply because the man has always had insomnia and was usually awake when the kids came in. So the son would come in after a dance or something and they'd sit and talk, and those were the best times of all. There's an intimacy in the night, and you can say things to each other at that hour that would be impossible at three o'clock in the afternoon.

The home movie of the mind flashes on the afternoon the father sat in a church hall and watched a group of teenagers on a stage in the throes of rehearsal. His son played the bass guitar and also sang. Something called "Proud Mary." Again there was that marvel and the mystery. Your children are constantly surprising you—suddenly he's up there on the stage, cool and in command, singing, a stranger.

And so it goes. The driver's license. The first big prom. The time he decided to grow a mustache. College and summer vacations and pumping gas. All the skis and skates and hiking gear. The first car and the first full-time job. And then the lovely girl who sends his heart askew.

All this goes through the father's mind as the day approaches. Ah, that day. When the father and the mother are no longer at stage center in the lives of their sons and daughters but stand a little to the side.

And the differences.

The father of the bride gives his daughter away but the father of the groom just sits there in the pew. The father of the bride dances with his daughter but the father of the groom can only stand and watch.

But there comes a time when the bride and groom are about to depart and the man watches them go. The boy he knew long ago has vanished and a man now strides toward the future. There's a special music in the father's heart—a song of hope and happiness and love. He heard this music once before when a certain bride danced in his arms.

And maybe there's not much difference between the father of the bride and the father of the groom after all.

January 6, 1978

Home

Saying Thank You

THE TIME CAME FOR THE MAN TO SIT DOWN AND WRITE SOME THANK YOU notes, and he selected a moment when the house was subdued and wrote them all in one long session at the desk.

He had made out a list in advance and checked the names off as he finished each note, hoping they conveyed what they never can convey, naturally: true appreciation.

There was one name left at the bottom of the list and he pondered it awhile. The name was "Mom." So he reached for the notepaper and set it before him and sat there and wondered: How do you say thanks to your mother?

He had sent her countless cards through the years, of course. On Mother's Day and at Christmastime and on her birthday. He even sent her Valentine Day cards along with carnations. She loves carnations. But he had never sat down and written her a simple Thank You note.

He has seen his own children growing up and is aware of the beautiful continuity of life, the weather of the family that delights the seasons of time. Just as long ago he sat with his own father late into the night and sipped cool beer, so has he sat with his own son and sipped the beer. And just as his own son sends cards to his mother on special occasions, so has he. But never a Thank You note.

And he realized that it's almost impossible to send a standard note of appreciation to your mother. How can you say: Thanks for the gift, Mom, it was really great? How can you thank her for one gift while neglecting, oh, a hundred, a thousand, gifts through the years? Not all of them were gifts that came in packages with bright ribbons and carefully selected wrapping paper.

The man is a writer and earns his living at the typewriter. Words are his business. But he knows that there are times when words are paltry offerings. So he turned from the desk and looked out the window and thought of the years and he realized that his mother, more than anyone else, led him to his profession. The man had been blessed with fine teachers across the years and excellent editors as well. But the woman he calls mother was there before he even knew he wanted to write, when he was only dimly aware of an impulse toward expression.

For instance, when he was just a kid, he'd arrive home from a Saturday afternoon movie, some minor western, maybe, with Ken Maynard, or a cops-and-robbers thing with Chester Morris; and he would tell her about the movie, scene by scene, summoning all the dialogue he could remember. She'd sit there in her chair, or maybe she was doing the dishes or the ironing or something, and she'd listen. This was her great art: listening. She never tired of hearing those movie stories. It wasn't until a long time later that the man realized she probably had been bored to tears, wondering: Will he ever stop talking? But instead listening, intent, reacting to the twists and turns of plot. And the boy got great satisfaction out of this. He was becoming a writer without knowing it. He was being a story-teller, even though they were other people's stories. Later, he would tell his own.

His mother was also his major audience. Oh, he showed stuff he had written to his teachers in school and he wrote for the school paper, the way aspiring writers do, but he showed her the writing in which he risked absurdity, took chances, walked the tightrope, knowing she would forgive any misstep that would hurtle him below. Once, long before, she, too, had written, and she understood the beauty and the terror of trying to get it down on paper. And so she revealed another great art of hers: reading his stories and poems with a sense of awe and wonder. Let the teachers criticize his writing at school; he needed that if he was to learn. But he also needed the loving audience, the reader who would forgive him everything, pardon his excesses and overlook his flaws and defects. She was that kind of reader at a time when he needed that kind of reader.

Ah, those days of boyhood when longing rose with him in the morning and never left his side. He would haunt the library and return with armloads of books, spilling them on the kitchen table. During Depression winters, he lay on the floor near the black Barstow stove and flew the trapeze with Saroyan's daring young man and stalked the streets of yearning with Thomas Wolfe's young writer seeking fame and fortune. He would scribble something on a scratch pad on the kitchen table and rush to read it to this beautiful woman who was not only his mother but someone who listened and shook her head with wonder and said: That's fine, that's just fine. You're going to be a real writer someday, mark my words.

* * *

So now he marks her words. She was the prophet who gave him dreams, the gentle sorceress who dazzled him with hope, who fed him more than food at the kitchen table: she fed him the marvelous food of possibility. He was a scrawny kid with a heart full of longing and a head full of dreams. He wanted to translate everything he saw and heard and felt into words leaping on the page. How could he ever do it? But you can, she said, you can.

Sitting at the desk, he realized the futility of writing her the polite, ordinary Thank You note.

He wrote this instead.

June 15, 1977

Away

A Day to Last Forever

"I'll take Manhattan,
the Bronx and Staten Island, too . . ."

—Lorenz Hart

MAYBE NOT THE BRONX, NOT THESE DAYS, BECAUSE THEY ARE TRASHING THE apartment buildings or burning them down. Staten Island, of course, looms offshore, unseen, although the ferry still plows its way across the harbor in the shadow of the Statue of Liberty.

We stood on the pedestal at the base of the statue and saw the Staten Island ferry, and it was such a clear day, the sun winking on the waves, that if you looked north past the skyline it seemed as if you could see the Bronx after all, or perhaps you could see forever, the way another song says.

Anyway, it was a perfect spring day in New York, stunningly bright, the way it happens occasionally in Manhattan. The young lovers strolled hand in hand, even to the base of Miss Liberty. We saw the statue this time through the eyes of a certain child and we were all properly awed at its size and immensity. And she asked the question we couldn't answer: Why is the statue green? We wondered if time and the elements had given it this hue—or what?

Later, we strolled through the streets of Chinatown as springtime continued its benevolence of sunshine and sweetness. The young and the old were out. Ancient men with skin like parchment stood on the corners conversing. The hustle of traffic provided the sound track. Because Chinatown is close to the Bowery, the derelicts wandered by now and then, and an ageless guy—was he twenty-eight or sixty-eight? —in a mottled overcoat asked us for a coin. Eyes red-rimmed, flesh like a worn copper coin. There is something in the eyes that you only see in the derelicts, something that compels you to reach into your pocket. He shuffles away after thanking us at embarrassing length, as if we had thrown him a life preserver and not just loose change. Maybe we had.

The uptown bus bumps along the avenue and the old jazz tunes ring in the brain as always on a New York bus. "Let Me off Uptown" and "Take the A Train" and all the Ellington and Krupa stuff that captures the excitement of it all. A young woman sits there, a child of four or five on her lap. She says to the child: "My ear is ringing." And the child places his ear to her ear. "I can't hear anything," the child says. The mother laughs, delighted, and hugs the child close. "Of course you can't," she says.

Central Park shimmers in the sunshine and we ride a hansom cab. The drivers wear top hats and are gentle with their crops. Our horse is named Cindy and she clops slowly along, the hoofbeats lazy as she carries us through the park. A spring day in Central Park should be preserved under glass forever so that nobody ever grows old or dies. Again we are surrounded by the young lovers, and they lounge on the lawn, seeing no one but themselves, creating their own small islands of longing. The bike riders are here and the joggers—it's funny how the bike riders seem content and the joggers agonized—and the kids are on skateboards. They whiz by us and the horse takes its time. The drivers tip their top hats to each other as they pass and everything is gentle and easy.

Everywhere in the park there is music. A brass band plays in a clearing and the clash of brass fills the air as we pass. A bit later, we hear the sounds of guitar, bass, and drum, muted but clear, the sounds caressing the air. The driver helps us down from the carriage, and the horse, of palomino color, stands patiently by while the child, who loves horses with a passion, gently strokes him. We stand there a moment as she says good-bye to Cindy and then we stroll toward the zoo.

New York City on a dazzling day in spring makes you feel sentimental and happy, but somehow there's a poignancy in it all. You want the day never to end. Even though the legs protest the walking. So you sit, in the beer garden near the zoo, and sip the cold brew while munching—what else?—roasted peanuts.

Later, Fifth Avenue is thronged as we stroll toward St. Patrick's. We pass the famous stores, Tiffany and Saks and all the others, and pause for a moment to linger. The buildings vault to the sky. The traffic creates jazz in our ears and I hear echoes of Gershwin that nobody else hears, but that's all right. We step into the majesty of St. Pat's and a choir is singing, the voices tumbling around us. A strange scent fills the air and then we pin it down—burning candles. Small candles burn at all the sanctuaries the way they no longer burn in churches we know. The smell of a thousand burning candles somehow sends purity across the air. But, of course, that's only an illusion of mine.

Such sweet illusions, however. They are a part of New York City on a day in springtime, a day that will never end no matter what the clocks or calendars say.

May 4, 1977

The Lady with a Torch

THIS ONE IS GOING TO BE CORNY AND PATRIOTIC AND SENTIMENTAL, SO IF YOU don't like that kind of stuff, you can turn to the comic pages or read the latest scandal by Jack Anderson or something.

Maybe it's all connected with Thanksgiving, this feeling I had, although the Thanksgiving part came later.

Anyway, there we were, aboard a great ship at a pier in Manhattan as dusk arrived like soot sprinkled over ship and shore, softening the sharp edges of things. From where we stood at the rail, we could see the Manhattan skyline, a million lights winking on, pinpricks in a curtain holding off the night. The ship moved, imperceptibly at first because the waters of the Hudson River are calm and barely rippling. The ship backed out of the dock with surprising ease, the way you'd back your car out of the driveway. As we made our way down the river to the harbor, the skyline receded a bit, enough to give us a better perspective.

New York is always a marvel to behold, its vaulting towers reaching toward the sky, almost touching the stars, so that they sometimes give the illusion of being July Fourth sparklers. You can view the skyline at a distance as you slant into LaGuardia by plane from Boston. Or you can walk the concrete canyons of the city and look up, look up, stretching your eye to its limits. I have always been in love with New York City, despite all the bad publicity and the tendency to downgrade the place. I have loved it for champagne at the Palm Court and good conversation at the Algonquin and strolling the streets where Thomas Wolfe stalked late at night in an ecstasy of longing and creation.

But the other evening, at dusk, on the deck of a ship heading out toward the Atlantic, as the chill of November caused you to hug your companion closely, there was a magnificence and a poignancy I had never known before.

We were like children, really, having left behind and on shore whatever sophistication we had gathered through the years. We oh'd and ah'd about the view, rushing from one side of the ship to the other, to see New Jersey blinking at us on one side (I still don't know port from starboard) and Manhattan on the other.

And then it happened.

We were moving calmly, darkness almost complete now, when suddenly someone said:

"There she is."

And there she was.

The Statue of Liberty.

Arm raised, torch held high, caught in the glow of a thousand lights, radiant in the dark. Now, we had all seen the statue a thousand times before, in movies and newsreels. We had caught glimpses of her on countless visits to Manhattan, although I had never taken the tourist trip to Bedloe's Island, where she resides in her lonely splendor. Who hasn't learned that verse in school—"Give me your tired, your poor, your huddled masses yearning to breathe free . . ." Ah, but that was years ago, wasn't it, when we were kids and believed everything we read in history books and were convinced that George Washington really did cut down the cherry tree.

But then you grow up and find out that the history books sometimes colored the times and the events, and disillusion often creeps in. We become blasé and casually cynical. And it's important to act nonchalant.

A moment arrives, however, when you are a small figure on a huge ship moving through the darkness toward distant shores, leaving your home behind, and out of the night there is suddenly the towering figure of that statue, leaping out of the history books into your life. Your breath catches, and there's an odd sensation in your chest.

And this is the corny part—suddenly, you love your country. You think of the millions who have passed by this statue—not only your tired and poor but everyone—and you are swept by a strange emotion, impossible to describe, incredibly sweet and lonely and—funny, mixed in with it is a kind of homesickness. Homesickness? Yes. And I can't explain why.

It's good to go away sometimes, if only because coming back is so sweet. On a sun-drenched morning, a few days later, the ship headed toward Manhattan. Out of the porthole I saw the Staten Island ferry plowing its way through the water to the mainland. My breath fogged the porthole window and I stepped away. And after a while, there she was again. The lady with the torch. Radiant in the morning, benevolent in the sunshine. I felt the sweetness again, this time mixed with a sense of going home. And laugh, if you want to, but I murmured "Thanks."

"Did you say something, hon?" she called from the dressing table.

"I'll tell you later," I said.

And I stood at the porthole watching the statue until it was time to go up for breakfast.

November 24, 1976

Las Vegas: Dark and Bright

THE HARD-EYED MEN ARE AT THE CRAPS TABLE BUT THE ACTION IS TOO SWIFT and complex to the amateur eye. The blackjack game is easier and more dramatic to follow.

The thing is to stand unobtrusively behind a player and play in your mind the cards that tumble to the table in swift succession.

The dealer sends the eight of diamonds across the table. The second card is a four of hearts. Then the queen of clubs. Fold.

The action is constant in the casino, from the little hours of the night when the players seem tireless as you return from a late show, to midmorning when you walk through the place on the way to breakfast.

Time has taken a holiday. There are no clocks. The casinos are seasonless, without weather. No one knows whether the sun shines outside or whether darkness has fallen and the fountains dance in the gathering dusk.

The slot machines are everywhere, of course. In fact, it has become a cliché now to point out that the machines are the first thing to greet you in Las Vegas as you emerge from the plane and enter the terminal. Ah, the slots. Those beckoning arms. The sudden shower of coins. The discovery of a hot machine, dispensing quarters like candy to a child. Bill Cosby says that his wife, who is otherwise normal, was seized with sudden wrath one morning when she entered the casino and found that someone was playing "her" machine, the machine that had been so good to her the night before.

Las Vegas is a kind of madness and it is divided into many parts. The visitors choose the part that fits a need or a desire. The gaming tables or the shows or some of both. But there is another Las Vegas, the one the visitor seldom sees, and this is the Las Vegas where people live and parents belong to the PTA and take out books at the public library and serve as lectors at church on Sunday.

A sedate middle-aged lady says that her daughter is a dealer at the Flamingo and her husband runs the baccarat game at Caesar's Palace. To her family, the strip is an industry, the way paper is to Fitchburg and plastics to Leominster.

Mario Puzo, who wrote *The Godfather,* writes about the dark side of the place in *Inside Las Vegas.* He takes us inside the neon wilderness to the world of gambling. He writes that Las Vegas is the big bet won, the miracle happening.

The casual visitor sips slowly at whatever delights he finds in Las Vegas but Puzo deals with the compulsive side of the place. Where everything is geared to games. Where Frank Sinatra is revered by the hotel owner because he will raise the "drop" of the casino more than any other entertainer; where Elvis Presley, who was the biggest draw in the history of the town, had no appeal for the high-rolling customers; where Barbra Streisand is a flop. In other words, the fans of Streisand skip the gaming tables, so who needs Streisand in the place? That's the way the owners see it.

Las Vegas is the insomniac's heaven because it never sleeps. One of the burdens the insomniac carries is loneliness. It is the loneliest thing in the world to be wide awake at three in the morning while the rest of the world slumbers. The loneliness is so sharp there's an ache in it. But in Las Vegas there is no three o'clock in the morning. Darkness falls when the sun drops behind the mountains in the west, but night never comes to the strip.

There is a constant fascination for the onlooker. The ceaseless games are irresistible. The dealers are like robots, most of them expressionless, their motions as automatic as the slot machines. Sometimes you sense a kind of bond between player and dealer. The give-and-take provides a link, a touching, that is not physical but almost spiritual. Then the player loses the final chip or silver dollar and moves on. The dealer deals, the cards fall on the table. And the brief kinship is over. Or did it actually exist?

At the craps table, the players sign the checks for $100 or $1000 and you linger there, fascinated, aware of an urgency in the air. The dice dance on the table and come to rest. Sometimes a howl erupts from a table where someone has scored. And the slot machines whirl. It is not merely legend but true that the older ladies with blue hair play the slots steadily, their coins in a paper cup. They don't even turn at the howl but keep on playing.

Another legend: There was once a bomb scare in a casino—and nobody vacated the premises. Puzo said the legend has basis in fact and writes about it this way:

> In all the arguments about . . . gamblers, the discussion narrows down to what game holds the biggest fascination for players—blackjack, shooting craps, roulette, baccarat or the slots. The argument is finally resolved by this true story.
>
> At the Sahara Hotel years ago, with the casino jammed with gamblers of all types, an anonymous threat came to the management that a bomb had been planted. The Casino Manager got on the loudspeaker system and announced: "A bomb threat has been received; please vacate the casino." Nobody moved. Five minutes later, the Casino Manager announced again: "Please, everybody, leave the casino. A bomb threat has been received."
>
> The blackjack players were the first to go, then the crap shooters (it could be the dice were cold that night), then the baccarat players; finally, the roulette players left. But the slot machines kept on whirring and flashing. The players kept thrusting in their coins. Out of the thousand players only four would leave their machines. Luckily, the bomb threat proved to be a hoax.

* * *

So you watch the hard-eyed gamblers at the big tables and marvel at their compulsion and their thousand-dollar checks. But, it turns out, the everyday people with a handful of dimes or quarters at the slot machines are the real gamblers after all, chasing the dream, the miracle, the silver shower that assuages the spirit but only for a moment or two.

November 11, 1977

Bar Conversation—and an Ending

LET'S SEE, WHERE WAS I? OH YES, VACATION—AND HOW THE BEAUTY OF IT all is fracturing routine, breaking the ordinary cycle of events. Without guilt. I mean, like staying up till all hours—2:30 in the morning, for instance—which can be done frequently, but during vacation you can stay up without the responsibilities of tomorrow awaiting, guilt lifted from your shoulders. And during vacation there always comes that time when you seek anonymity and so you drive to another city —it doesn't matter where as long as you're a stranger—and you stroll the sidewalks, linger on a park bench, wander the library, visit the book and record stores—all of this as if you're invisible.

On occasion, I am drawn to neighborhood side-street bars and their dim coolness and ask for a bottle of beer and sit quietly while the life of the bar goes on. It's a joy to watch a bartender who is a craftsman, just as it's a joy to watch any expert at work, whether he's a short-order cook or a shoe repairer. These are the everyday artists, although I'm speaking now only of those who take pride in their work. Anyway, in this small cool bar in that distant city, the bartender was an artist, knowing his customers, anticipating their needs, responding to a quiet nod, a raised eyebrow, a flickering finger, and pouring the stuff smoothly and expertly.

Conversation has a distinct flair and flavor in a bar, unlike conversation elsewhere, and it touches on the Red Sox and politics and then they begin to talk about Manny. "Hey, where's Manny been anyway?" someone asked. And the bartender, pondering the question as he poured another beer, said, "I dunno. He hasn't been around." And somebody said: "Maybe he's on vacation. He always goes to the

Cape." And the first fellow said: "But four, maybe five, weeks. Manny don't get that kind of vacation." Big pause in the bar. "Hey, maybe he's dead," somebody said, in that half-humorous, tentative way of saying something that you don't really believe, but then who knows? Who knows? "Naw, not Manny," the first fellow said.

Perhaps nobody else noticed the remark and the conversation turned to other topics and I was dying for a cigarette—it has been six years now since I quit smoking, but I always crave a cigarette in a bar —and I thought of Manny. Manny must be something, really. Maybe he's dead, someone said. And somebody else answered, "Naw, not Manny." Hey, Manny, who are you, anyway, that you wouldn't be dead like anyone else? I finished the bottle and left the bar and nobody said good-bye, because I was transient, temporary. And as I opened the door to step out into the street, I felt like saying: "Give my regards to Manny." But didn't. I never make those dramatic gestures I long to make.

It was during vacation that the tenth anniversary of the death of Ernest Hemingway occurred—how time passes too quickly. And, of course, I turned again to *A Farewell to Arms* and *The Sun Also Rises,* cruising the pages, picking up a line here and a phrase there and, of course, his endings—how Hemingway could end his novels—"Isn't it pretty to think so?" And: "After a while I went out and left the hospital and walked back to the hotel in the rain." Some of the cruelest words I have encountered are the final words of Carlos Baker's biography of Hemingway. They had to be cruel, of course, to create their impact. He tells of how Hemingway on the Sunday morning of July of 1961 awoke early and went to the basement storage room and chose a double-barreled Boss shotgun with a tight choke.

> He took some shells from one of the boxes in the storage room . . . and climbed the basement stairs. If he saw the bright day outside, it did not deter him. He crossed the living room floor to the front foyer . . . with oak-paneled walls and a floor of linoleum tile. He had held for years to his maxim: "il faut (d'abord) durer." Now it had been succeeded by another: "il faut (après tout) mourir." The idea, if not the phrase, filled all his mind. He slipped in two shells, lowered the gun butt carefully to the floor,

leaned forward, pressed the twin barrels against his forehead just above the eyebrows, and tripped both triggers.

But naw, not Manny.

July 13, 1971

Musi, the Steward

I THINK ABOUT MUSI A LOT THESE DAYS.

I think of him when the snow falls and the world resembles one of
those small glass scenes that you shake to send the snowflakes tumbling.

I think about him as I walk past huge mounds of snow piled high at
the roadsides and huddle against the wind.

And I wonder about him and whether he will ever get to Switzerland.

To begin with, it's hard to picture Musi in Switzerland, that moun-
tainous place of snow and ski. He obviously belongs to other lands,
places of sunshine and water. He told us he was Indonesian and called
his homeland a place of a thousand islands. And his face is stamped
with the sun of countless seasons.

We met him on board a huge ship easing its way down the Hudson
River toward the Atlantic. We confronted him as we entered our
stateroom and he greeted us with a smile as bright as a sunrise.

"Hello, I am Musi," he said. He said he would be our steward for
the cruise. He was short, uniformed in blue and red, and that smile
was always there.

"If you need anything," he said, "call me. . . ."

The world of big ships is an alien world where you learn even to
walk differently. Musi was our guide. He was always on the move,
from stateroom to stateroom, but somehow he found the time to
linger for a while and talk.

He was both visible and invisible. We felt his presence as we came
and went . . . a basket of fruit would appear on the side table and
we knew he had been there. Once, when one of the travelers didn't

feel up to par, Musi appeared with a silver tray of tea and toast and apples.

One night when the sea was rough and the ship tumbled in the waves, he was a comforting presence.

"This nothing," he said, smiling away. "A big good ship like this . . . no fear." And he told of other sailings when the big good ship stormed its way through hurricane and typhoon and always made it to calm waters.

We docked in a harbor when we arrived at our destination, and a ferry took passengers and crewmen ashore. We looked out and saw Musi high above, on the boat deck, his line dangling into the sea. Later he told us that he enjoyed fishing. He liked fish and rice. "Rice," he said, "best of all. Your food," he said, indicating the dining room, where the gourmet menus waited, "too rich." He rolled his *r*'s as if he had long practiced those *r*'s.

He told us of other voyages he had made and of the fabulous people who had been in his charge. Jerry Lewis and Ella Fitzgerald and Mickey Rooney. He said that people on first-time cruises are the most pleasant to deal with because everything is new and they appreciate it all. The repeaters are demanding . . . they compare one cruise with another . . . one ship with another. And those famous people? "One man . . . famous movie star . . . warm milk he liked at bedtime . . . three times I go below because milk not right . . . too warm . . . too cool . . . three times . . ." And he shrugged, the smile returning. "All kinds of people on a cruise . . . some nice, some not so nice. . . . Like life. . . ."

You have a tendency to become sentimental when a journey is ending, particularly an ocean voyage, when you have lived for a time with people in a special world cut off from home. Casual acquaintances suddenly become good friends and casual friendships are suddenly cherished.

We stayed up late one night toward the end, talking to Musi. It had been a long day but his smile persisted.

"You're such a happy fellow," I said. "Are you really so happy all the time?"

The smile disappeared.

"Happy outside," he said, indicating his lips. "But not inside," touching his chest.

"I have no wife, no home, no . . . career." The *r*'s in career rolled magnificently, if sadly. "I was teacher in my homeland . . .

but not enough money . . . no chance to make good. So, I come
on ship, work. . . ."

"Where do you spend vacations?"

"No vacation," he said. "Seven days work . . ."

"The ship is going in next month for repairs, I heard. Won't you
have time off?"

"No," he said. "We work. Scrub clean."

And then, as if to reassure us, the smile appeared again. "Hey,
good life, this. Better than homeland. But lonesome, too. Better
than homeland but still not home. I travel the world . . . all over
. . . all countries . . ."

"Which place was best?"

He paused, thinking.

"Most places good. But now in port, I stay on ship." He paused
again. "Someday I live in Switzerland, maybe. Clean. Snow. High
mountains."

I thought of Switzerland, an inland country, landlocked.

"No ocean," I said.

He smiled. "No ocean."

We docked late in the morning and the ship was scheduled to sail
that same afternoon for another destination, other ports along the
way. Musi would be aboard, smiling away, bringing the tea and toast,
turning down the blankets, bestowing his benevolence.

I wonder if he will ever make it to Switzerland, where no sea kisses
its shores.

January 21, 1977

In the Nation's Capital

I AM, BY NATURE, AN INCURABLE OPTIMIST.

When someone sees the bottle as half empty, I view it as half full.

I never believe the bad-weather forecasts.

And I always expect the parade to start on time.

My favorite cartoon is the one that shows two prisoners manacled
high on a wall with no obvious means of escape and one of the
prisoners says: "Now, here's my plan. . . ."

And because I am an undiscouraged optimist, with a plan always afoot, I paused outside the White House in the nation's capital in a drenching downpour the other day and looked up at the second-floor windows.

I was soaked to the skin. We had stood for more than an hour in the rain, waiting to get into the White House, and we had dripped puddles through the Green Room and the Blue Room and the State Dining Room. A quick tourist trip.

Now I stood there, still soaked, the rain lacerating my upturned face.

"What are you doing?" someone asked.

"I'm checking to see if Jimmy Carter might be looking out at us."

That's the kind of optimist I am, to suppose that the President of the United States might peek out of the window at the exact moment I looked up.

As it turned out, he didn't appear and I had to rush to catch up to the others. But the prospect had not been entirely farfetched. The flag was flying on the White House, which meant he was in town. It was only 10:30, and it was possible that he had left the Oval Office to have a coffee break with Rosalynn. I don't know. To me, anything is possible.

In fact, my presence at the White House that morning was implausible in itself. That's because I made a decision some years ago that I wouldn't stand in line anymore. I figured that life was too brief and fleeting to waste time standing in line. Oh, I don't mind standing behind a few people at the bank or the supermarket or the movies. What I mean is a long, long line. Like at a world premiere. Or a crucial Red Sox-Yankee game at Fenway Park. Or an around-the-block line for a standing-room-only Broadway play.

Not for me. Not anymore. No thanks.

Another thing I swore off long ago was the guided tour. I swore off guided tours in the eighth grade when I was shepherded along with what seemed like a thousand other kids through a historical tour of Boston. I think we were safety patrols or something. Anyway, we were herded here and there, kept in line, jostled, trampled by somebody walking behind, yelled at by the chaperones, who must have needed barrels of tranquilizers for the next three months. As far as I was concerned, it was a nightmare. I have a dim memory of being

forced up the stairs of the Bunker Hill Monument while claustrophobia rang alarm bells in my body.

Never again, I said, even at that tender age.

But suddenly there I was on a bus tour of Washington, D.C.,
standing in endless lines at the White House and Mount Vernon and
the Capitol building, among others.

The fact of my presence there was not amazing—everyone should
at one time or another visit our nation's capital, of course—but the
truly amazing thing was that I was thoroughly enjoying the visit, bus
trip, lines, and all.

Why?

Because despite all my protests about waiting in line and the rest of
it, I am constantly besieged by sentiment and patriotism. Good old-
fashioned patriotism, that the pseudosophisticates and the cynics
shrug off. But there it is. I figure that I, too, am cynical and I think
about the raise Congress sneaked for itself and the scandals and such
—but suddenly we are standing in Arlington Cemetery at the Tomb
of the Unknowns, watching the changing of the guard. The young
men stand at attention, erect as knifeblades. They march in cadence.
Taps sound from the silver bugle, the notes melting in the morning
sunshine. I am moved to tears. I clutch the hand of a child in my
own, hoping she sees the meaning of it all, that we still care for
tradition, that we honor our valiant dead, that this ritual among the
pale slabs of a cemetery symbolizes what is good and strong and yes,
sweet, in this nation of ours.

Later we stand at the gravesite of John Kennedy— "Dear Jack," as
Cardinal Cushing called him—and we look out toward the Washington Monument and the Capitol, all in a direct line. That night, we
look up in awe at the Lincoln Memorial and the winds of evening
sound like organ music in the heart, full of majesty, full of wonder.

Thus I go to Washington a cynic and return a patriot. Even if
Jimmy Carter didn't look out that White House window. . . .

April 8, 1977

Somehow, You Just Sit There

THE STRANGE THING IS THAT THE EVENTS OF YOUR PAST DON'T FLY THROUGH your mind and you don't panic, either. Somehow, you just sit there. Probably, it's because we have become accustomed to emergency, drama, and crisis in our lives, in the headlines and on the screens and even on the sidewalks, and so we are somehow prepared when an emergency affects us personally. Or probably there is, after all, something in a human being that responds in splendid fashion in crisis, an adrenaline of the spirit that pumps courage into us when it's needed.

Specifically, I am speaking of a flight to the Midwest and how we touched down at Cleveland and then took off for Fort Wayne, Indiana. Frankly, I felt a small radar signal of dismay when I learned about the Fort Wayne stopover. This was my first flight and everything had gone beautifully since the takeoff at Boston.

But Fort Wayne hadn't been listed on our itinerary—we had originally been scheduled to fly directly to our destination from Cleveland. Now there was an extra takeoff and landing ahead. However, life is made up of the unexpected and you learn to accept it all.

Thus I wasn't really that surprised when the pilot's voice came over the intercom a few minutes after we had left the Cleveland airport:

"I have been informed that a piece of rubber was found on the runway after we departed from Cleveland and there's a possibility it may be part of our tire." He assured us that there was nothing to be worried about, but he asked us to fasten our seat belts again, as he was planning to proceed to Fort Wayne and fly 500 feet above the airport to allow observers to check the condition of the tires.

After a while the descent began above the checkerboard farms of Indiana.

The passengers were quiet, although people exchanged uneasy glances. I looked at that child of six and she looked back with innocence and trust in her eyes. Perhaps she hadn't been listening when the pilot made the announcement. The stewardess had given her "Future Stewardess" wings and she was still enchanted by them. She'd also been given two lengths of string and a guide to knot-making, and this had diverted her. Whatever it was, she displayed no alarm. Her mother checked her seat belt and held her hand. This was fine with the child—she's going through an affectionate stage at the moment;

loves everybody in the world but always and especially her mother, of course.

After what seemed a long time, the pilot came on the intercom again and acknowledged that, yes, that was a piece of our tire back there at Cleveland. But there was no cause, really, for alarm. However, we would not go back to Fort Wayne but would proceed to our destination.

He explained that we'd be landing in fifteen minutes or so. He said that he would de-accelerate the engines very quickly and this would make a particularly loud noise. Or words to that effect. Frankly, I wasn't taking notes and my knowledge of jets and engines is minimal anyway.

The waiting is the hard part. The knowledge that you are powerless to help yourself. A child of fate, part of a design you cannot change. You tell yourself that nothing could possibly happen, that a small piece of rubber could not possibly wreck a plane. You urge yourself to stop exaggerating the danger: this is everyday business for the pilot. You glance out the window at the flat midwestern landscape and notice that all the barns are red. You feel that you have to point this out to the child, for some reason. Everyone is so calm. The sun shimmers on the wings. You wonder if the plane might nosedive if it stops too fast on the runway. Stop exaggerating. Nothing's going to happen. It happens to other people, not you.

Then there's that change in speed, that quick downward movement that causes the ears to block until you swallow. The plane touches down and the landscape races by and a sudden shattering noise erupts. There has never been such a noise. And it goes on . . . and on . . . unendingly, as the plane keeps moving . . . Will it ever stop? The noise mounts, reaches a crescendo that makes you wince, and then it stops, like a door slamming, and at the same time the plane slows down. You glance outside and see the fire trucks pulling up alongside—just like the movies, you think ridiculously. The jet stops. No longer moving. A collective sigh of relief sweeps the plane.

The passengers erupt in a burst of applause. It's as if we had all been slumbering, subdued or numbed by danger, and now we awaken. The applause releases the tension, and it's not only for the pilot who landed us safely but somehow a celebration of our own.

Complete strangers look at each other with—I don't know—affection, maybe. We have shared a moment. The fire trucks follow us but they are symbols of safety now, not harbingers of danger. We taxi to the air terminal and the engines die. We have arrived at our destination. We are safe and sound. For some reason, I want to hug the child and everyone else. Life is so incredibly sweet, isn't it?

November 13, 1973

The Loneliness of the Long-distance Traveler

I KNEW I WAS IN TROUBLE WHEN THE CLERK AT THE AIRLINES DESK ASKED THE man in front of me: "How much do you weigh?"

"Two-oh-five," he answered, after hesitating just a bit.

I hesitated, too, when she asked me the same question a moment later. Now it was my turn to ask a question, although I dreaded the answer: "How big is this plane, anyway?"

"Oh, we have two sizes," she said. "The big one and the small."

"I hope I get the big one," I said, wondering if she could see the desperation in my eyes.

"The big one is eight passengers," she explained. "The small one is six." She didn't seem to notice my shudder. "You'll enjoy it," she added. "The plane never goes above ten thousand feet—you have a magnificent view all the way."

I ended up on the six-passenger job, trapped in a small, wobbling aircraft because there was no other way to keep my appointment in Cleveland. I didn't enjoy the view of the Ohio landscape; I was too much involved in holding on whenever we flew into a cloud bank— which was often. I kept wondering: What am I doing here?

Here's what I was doing there: I was on a business venture that took me for the space of five weeks or so through the East and Midwest, north as far as Toronto, south as far as New Orleans. Travel brings marvelous moments: dinner in the Pump Room of the Ambassador Hotel in Chicago as notes from the baby grand anoint the air; sunset on Lake Ontario as a boat knifes through the darkening water; powdered sugar sprinkled on beignets in a French Quarter bistro while the crowd hustles and bustles outside the window; saluting the statue of Stan Musial outside Busch Stadium in St. Louis as the excitement mounts before the umpire cries, "Play ball." . . . And there's the wonder of arriving in a great city at dusk, the lights of Montreal or Washington, D.C., winking seductively as you drive from the airport, the symphony of horns and brakes and police whistles creating strange music in your ears.

And yet, and yet. There is something else, too. Something under the surface does not reveal itself until the third or fourth week—especially when you are traveling alone. I first sense it in a wonderful hotel restaurant in Cleveland where the martini is stinging, the filet mignon juicy and tender, the service swift and impeccable. Glancing around the room, I observe three other men dining alone, studying their food seriously, as if certain answers could be found on the plate. The men look familiar to me but I can't recall their faces. Then I realize the truth. I do not know their faces but I recognize the three-piece suits, the button-down shirts, the subdued ties, and I know that upstairs in the room are the bulging briefcases.

All along I have been dimly aware of these men in my travels, filing onto the commuter special at the end of the day, shirt collar wilting but tie still correctly knotted, the double Scotch, the briefcase sometimes flipped open and the pencil poised above the row of figures.

On a morning flight out of La Guardia for St. Louis, the man in the blue blazer and oxford-cloth shirt tells me he leaves every Monday morning and returns home late Thursday night. "I used to stay out till Friday but I got that turned around. Now I make local calls on Friday and I'm out only four nights." *Out* means away from home, a telephone call away from the wife and kids, who tell about emergencies or report cards on a long-distance line.

In the lobby of a big city hotel I find myself standing beside another man, both of us looking out the window into the twilit street. I enjoy city streets, absorbing the sights and sounds and the anonymity as well. I tell the man I'm thinking of taking a stroll.

"Don't," he says, tight-lipped, without turning his head. "Stay here in the hotel. Nobody goes wandering downtown here anymore—not after dark."

Instantly I am claustrophobic, feeling trapped there in a glittering hotel in the middle of a big city, unable to leave, a prisoner of the times in which we live. So I return to my room and make the daily phone call home—Renée has made it to the finals in the seventh-grade spelling bee, but I won't be home for the finals—and then I watch television and read awhile. And so to bed, after checking the weather forecast. I wake as usual at four o'clock in the morning, wondering not only where I am but who I am.

Thus the thing that surfaces is loneliness, an emotional soot that settles finally on the heart. You barely notice it in the brotherhood of the bar, where the drinks are swiftly poured and camaraderie is sudden, where the jukebox is loud and laughter is rampant. The cast of characters seldom changes: the garrulous guy whose conversation booms with punch lines, the charmer who flirts with the waitress and fails to notice that she obviously is not interested and probably has a migraine, the drinker who seeks nightly oblivion in the bottom of the glass, the solitary man still in suit and tie who winces at the loud talk and harassing jukebox but prefers this to the empty hotel room. . . .

And I am glad to be an observer, silent and watchful and untouched. I am not one of them, I tell myself. Next week, home again, the travels ended. A flood of warmth engulfs me and it doesn't come from the drink.

But a small voice inside me says: If your travels weren't over in a few days and you were doomed to stay *out,* on the road, going from city to city, forever, which would you be? I look around the lounge, see the faces and hear the voices, watch the guy who talks too much and the one who drinks too much and the charmer who flirts too much and the loner who is there but not there at the same time, and I wonder again who I am, even though it's not four o'clock in the morning.

I finish the beer, call for the check, leave the bar, and know that sleep will not come easily tonight.

July 1980

A Bit of Warmth in a Foreign Place

I AM STARTLED TO SEE THE OLD MAN THERE, SITTING IN THE BOOTH, THE plate containing his half-consumed dinner, a pleasant smile on his face as he regards us. The woman leads us to a table near the old man. She wears a polite smile: We are customers, travelers who have stopped for a bite to eat in her modest restaurant—so modest that she serves as both waitress and cook—and there is no recognition in her eyes.

But then, why should there be? We had stopped at her restaurant on the outskirts of Saint-Hyacinthe, in the Province of Quebec, a few miles from the Richelieu River, a year ago—almost to the day. Then we had wanted a quick bite to eat at noontime. The place was a fortunate choice, pure luck. We had found that the soup was home-made and so were the pies—raisin pies that my wife remembered from her childhood at her mother's table and hadn't eaten since.

So, a year ago we had happened on that tiny restaurant and had enjoyed a pleasant, on-the-road midday snack—soup, sandwich, pie. An old man sat nearby. He kept looking at us in a friendly fashion, his attention drawn by Renée, who last year was eleven.

Perhaps he heard my atrocious accent as I tried to pronounce the French selections on the menu. At any rate, he leaned over and said, "I have a small joke for you." He spoke in English, here in the heart of the province! The words carried a tinge of French, a softening of the syllables, a lyrical lilt.

Renée's curiosity was aroused. Her eyes flashed with anticipation. She has always been eager to take great gulps of the world, although she is frequently shy and tentative.

"This is the story," the old man said, "of a dog who is sitting on sandpaper. And someone comes by and says, 'How goes life with you?' And the dog says, 'Rough, rough.'" But he pronounced the word as *ruff-ruff*, like the barking of a dog, exploding into laughter at the same time.

We laughed with him, sharing a warm and friendly moment in a foreign place. He was delighted with our laughter.

We talked awhile before our food was served. He said he was a retired railroad man, having worked as an engineer in the States— "out of Boston, out of Detroit"—before coming back to his home in the province to live out his days. His black suit was neat and well pressed and shiny from many cleanings. A black beret lay on the table near his plate. We carried on the small talk of people meeting as strangers, coming together for a time, sharing an instant but transient camaraderie.

Finally he pushed his plate away and stood up. He rose from the table by degrees, the way it happens when you are no longer young. He beamed down at Renée. "See you later, alligator," he said.

Renée smiled politely but looked a bit puzzled.

"You don't know the reply?" he asked. "You're supposed to say, 'In a little while, crocodile.'"

Laughing, patting Renée on the head, pleased with the moment and the old joke, he made his way to the counter and the cash register, where the woman who was the cook and the waitress also assumed the role of cashier. He waved to us as he went out the door, still smiling.

Now it's a year later. We're in Canada again and we remember that modest eating place with the rich homemade soups and pies. Can we find it? I drive along Rue Girouard and the scene is familiar. There's the place by the side of the road—newly painted, yellow. It's like coming home again.

The same woman meets us as we enter and she leads us to a table. You won't believe this but it's true—she directs us to the same table we occupied a year ago. And there, at *his* same table, is the old man. We look at each other, astonished. This can't be. It only happens this way in books, and even in books this would be stretching things a bit.

"I'm sure it's him," says Renée, who has a memory as true and sharp as a knife edge.

We aren't alone in the restaurant with the old man; there are other customers. Two young women at a table, eating pizza, a child in a high chair between them. The child is a handsome, lively boy, three years old probably.

The woman takes our order. Again the homemade soups and pies. She goes off to the kitchen.

"Are you sure?" I ask Renée.

Now she's doubtful. After all, a year has passed. In the parade from eleven to twelve, a year can be a century.

The old man finishes eating and pushes back his plate. He rises slowly and walks toward the two young women and the baby. He bends over the boy. He speaks slowly and in exaggerated accents to the child.

My wife looks at us, astonished. She's the bilingual one in the family, able to speak and understand French. "It's the same joke," she whispers. And, sure enough, we hear the climax of the story: *ruff-ruff.*

When he returns, we hail him and tell him of the coincidence—how we were here a year ago and sat at this same table while he sat at his. We don't tell him that he had told the same joke last year, however. We chat awhile and he speaks again of his railroad days—"out of Boston, out of Detroit"—and again it's a pleasant moment in our travels.

He prepares to depart—"Don't let me disturb your meal"—and looks down at Renée. "See you later, alligator," he says.

Renée hesitates and then joins me as I say, "In a little while, crocodile."

He goes off, the beret on his head, the shine on his black suit still radiant, the smile on his face still revealing his delight.

The woman brings us the check and we tell her what has happened. She shares our amazement and amusement at this coincidence. In answer to our questions, she says that the old man has been coming to the restaurant almost every day for four or five years. He orders the same thing every day—the soup du jour, the hamburg steak with mashed potatoes, and whatever pudding she has prepared. In fact, he doesn't order the meal. She brings it to him automatically.

"He is a nice old man," she says in French, and my wife doesn't have to interpret for us this time. Her expression translates the words.

We leave the restaurant, well fed and refreshed, and fulfilled somehow. I'm not quite sure how. It's nice to find a bit of warmth in a cold season in a foreign country. Yet, I wonder why I keep thinking of that old man and whether he'll be there if we return and whether there will always be children to hear his little jokes.

See you later, alligator . . .

February 1980

All the Cities We Love

THE CHRISTIAN SCIENCE MONITOR CONDUCTED A POLL RECENTLY TO FIND OUT from its readers which cities were the most livable in the United States.

San Francisco won, hands down.

And Boston came in second.

Now, I've never been to San Francisco, although I feel as though I've visited the place because it's been the background for so many movies, including *Bullitt,* which had us chasing a car up and down those endless concrete hills with Steve McQueen.

But Boston is another thing altogether.

There are many memorable aspects to Boston and it's easy to fall in love with the place. A visitor always carries away pleasant memories—a stroll through the Public Gardens after luncheon at the Ritz where the pianist in the tux played the old show tunes—"Smoke Gets in Your Eyes" and "I've Got You Under My Skin"—while the attentive waiters hovered over the women with the blue hair and the diamond pendants.

Boston is a place of stunning moments: hustling up the narrow alley that leads to Locke-Ober's, that most superb of restaurants. Or arguing with the bossy waitresses at Durgin Park while eating the warm cornbread. Fighting your way through Filene's bargain basement. And who can forget that first dazzling performance of *Hair* at the Wilbur and drinking the dark beer in the glass steins afterward at Jake Wirth's?

I can remember strolling the storied streets of Beacon Hill and the quality of autumn sun on the old brick buildings. And the dazzle of summer sun on the golden dome of the State House.

Ah, Boston.

Another thing about Boston is its blend of the ancient and the modern. It's a place where you turn a corner and stumble upon an old cemetery with those slim slabs of stones, plunging you suddenly into another era, until a taxi horn shatters the moment and returns you to the cacophony of the 1970s.

This contrast is everywhere and it is captured beautifully in Copley Square, where the tower of glass that's the John Hancock Building thrusts toward the sky while the old Trinity Church sits sedately nearby.

There are a lot of things about Boston that are beautiful. But it occurred to me as I read the *Monitor* list, that the same standards apply to just about any city.

The *Monitor* editors said that some readers bypassed such cities as New Orleans and Seattle (actually, Seattle came in third) and chose their own home towns.

And who can blame them?

There's a reason for this. There's good and bad in every city, even the most beautiful of communities. Boston, of course, has its share of ugly spots, the Combat Zone and other streets where no one cares to venture after fall of night. There's also the ugliness of mood that erupts now and then and brings national guardsmen to the streets.

I guess emotion has a lot to do with the way people regard a city.

Because I ran as a boy through the streets of Leominster, my feeling for that city has always been nostalgic. I remember my lost youth there and the beautiful moments are also filled with a kind of ache and longing.

There was to me no more beautiful place on earth than the Leominster Public Library, the sun benevolent as it slanted in the windows while I first encountered Hemingway and Thomas Wolfe and Saroyan. I remember the way the librarians always whispered—Miss Wheeler and Miss Wedge and the others.

From an eighth-grade schoolroom I could see beyond the houses to Monoosnock Hill and dreamed, like the Wolfian hero, of places far away and of someday conquering them.

Ah, Leominster . . . those gatherings in Monument Square on Memorial Day and the long marches to the cemeteries, Doyle Field on a Saturday afternoon as the cheerleaders leaped while the quarterback scampered for the score . . . the big white house on the hill where the girl I worshiped from afar lived in rooms I would never occupy.

If Leominster is the city of the past, then Fitchburg is the city of here and now—and a different emotion is evoked. Now a child's hand is in mine as we stroll through the Upper Common, and she frolics at the fountain there.

I seldom walk Main Street without glancing up Hartwell Street to that four-columned house on Prichard Street. Or look down on the city from the top of Laurel Hill Cemetery, the quiet of that old cemetery in contrast to the hustle and bustle below.

Fitchburg is the place where you can encounter dapper, mustachioed George R. Wallace as he strolls jauntily along—a symbol of so much that is good about Fitchburg.

I have always loved Fitchburg at dusk when Main Street becomes a tunnel melting into the darkness, all the harsh edges softened.

Or early in the morning, when the sun sets on fire the eastern windows in the houses on Summer Street near the Bernardian Bowl.

*　*　*

Without the emotions, a city would only be wood and brick, concrete and glass. And that's why, as the editors of the *Christian Science Monitor* found out, so many of their readers named places no one ever heard of as the most beautiful cities in which to live.

They named them because those places represent home and love and memory to them.

And that's where beauty really starts, not in the architecture but in the heart.

September 16, 1975

Beginnings, Endings

IT WAS A TIME OF BEGINNINGS AND ENDINGS.

First of all, the place was filled with ghosts. And as ghosts are supposed to be, they were white and spooky and still. We saw them as we stalked the corridors of the place, this beautiful Wentworth-By-The-Sea, a relic of the Victorian era that looks out over the Atlantic at Portsmouth, New Hampshire.

On an October Sunday the sea was muted, gooseflesh as the wind rippled it. The water was the color of slate in the pale morning sun, and far islands in the distance looked like tumbled dominoes. The dunce cap that turned out to be a sailboat tilted in the wind.

Anyway, the wind hurried us inside, and as we walked the long, dim hallways the doors to many of the rooms were open. And that's when we saw the ghosts.

The waitress explained it all as she poured coffee for us in the dining room. "Let's see, this is Sunday," she said. She was gray-haired, pleasant, her voice echoing Maine, like the twang of a banjo string. "This is the last day of the season for the guests. Tomorrow, we close up and then Tuesday I head for Palm Beach, Florida." She said that she followed the sun. Semiretired now, a native of Maine, she lives in Florida during the winters and works two or three months at Wentworth during late summer and fall.

That was the secret of the ghosts, of course, the maids covering the furniture, the lamps, even the telephones with white sheets. Actually, they place the telephones on the bed and cover the bed. Thus the lamps and the bureaus loom like pale specters in the rooms and you glimpse them as you pass.

And it's an ending. Sad, too, of course, like most endings.

There are other ghosts in a place like Wentworth-By-The-Sea, the ghosts of other years, all the beautiful ladies and handsome men who have come and gone in the past century. By some fortunate circumstance we stayed in the "Governor's Suite," two huge rooms facing the harbor, blue velvet drapery, sofas and chairs of ancient, formal style. In the lamp glow of evening it's easy to imagine the past grandeur, the clopping of hoofs as the carriages pull up, the liveried doorman.

Wentworth-By-The-Sea is not a moveable feast like Hemingway's Paris. You leave it behind and head south on the shore road, rounding the curves for heart-catching glimpses of the sea. The summer crowds are gone and few people stroll the beaches. Those who do are bundled up in jackets and scarves. And yet the sea has never looked so beautiful, as if the sea were a gray bedspread and the invisible hands of a giant were lifting and ruffling it to make it smooth. Then we round the final curve and the sea is behind us. Highways loom ahead.

Endings, beginnings.

October 27, 1976

Follies and
Fancies

What Worries Him

KNOW WHAT WORRIES ME?

This is what worries me:

I pick up the *Times* and see a sample of handwriting—it's an advertising pitch for a new book—and the ad says the handwriting is that of a schizophrenic.

And the handwriting looks almost exactly like my own.

I worry about things like that.

I also worry because I never know what to do when the repair man comes. I mean, I don't know whether I should stand there and watch him work. Or whether I should leave him alone.

I couldn't care less about picking up repair tips. Yet I don't want the repairman to think I'm standing there checking up on him. On the other hand, I always feel self-conscious sitting in the den, reading a book and maybe drinking beer while he's working away in the kitchen.

And I never know whether I should offer him a beer or not.

One repairman was indignant, almost self-righteous when I offered him a drink.

Another emptied the can in two huge gulps.

And it wasn't even a hot day.

I don't know. The little things worry me. Leaves, for instance. We have seventeen trees on our property. I can hardly tell an oak from a maple and I didn't even know we had a pear tree until the fruit appeared that first year. But I like having seventeen trees.

Then the season changes and down come the leaves. In multitudes. The leaves are beautiful in all their hectic colors. They are beautiful when a child scoops up a few and arranges them in a bouquet for her mother. They are beautiful clinging to the hair of lovely girls frolicking on a sunny afternoon.

But eventually they have to be picked up.

Meanwhile, I worry about them. This year, I began worrying about them in September when they first began to fall. And I worried all through October and into November.

I told myself they formed a beautiful carpet—and why destroy that carpet by picking them up so soon? They looked great tumbling in the wind, creating crackling whirlpools.

I worried when they landed on my neighbor's lawn. I worried because, frankly, I was overjoyed. And then I felt guilty.

So we picked up the leaves one weekend—and the next worry was what the hell do you do with them once you've picked them up and the pile in the backyard grows higher? I'm still worrying about that.

I also worry because I worry about things other people don't seem to worry about.

For instance, I always worry that the gasoline going into the tank will overflow when the station attendant goes off to take care of another car after setting the hose on automatic.

I worry because I like the smell of shoe polish.

I worry because I can never remember which banks we have accounts in—and when I try to cash a check and the cashier asks if I have an account there, I hesitate and have to think about it, and I feel like a petty criminal.

I worry about seeing an Unidentified Flying Object. I don't want to see one because I know that I won't be able to keep quiet about it. I'll tell everybody and probably write about it—and it will lead to all sorts of complications. Whenever I hear a noise in the sky at night, I don't look up anymore.

I worry because I have played Bob Dylan's "Wigwam" about 5000 times—maybe 2000 in a row—and nobody else gets excited about it.

I also worry when I tell people what I'm worried about and they say, "Funny, I never worry about that."

I worry when I go to the doctor and he takes my blood pressure and then doesn't say anything. And I wonder if he's keeping some terrible secret from me.

I want to ask him about it to be reassured and then I think, "What if . . ."

I also worry when I have a prescription filled and the pharmacist says, "We'll have to send away for this." I worry because I wonder if I have contracted a disease so rare that the medicine isn't even kept in stock.

I worry when people take me seriously when I'm trying to be funny and think I'm being funny when I'm being serious.

I worry because sometimes I'm not sure myself.

Like today.

And I keep thinking of that handwriting sample.

November 15, 1973

Why He's Not Running

I HAVE DECIDED NOT TO RUN FOR MAYOR THIS YEAR.

And I am not going to be a candidate for president next year.

There are a lot of reasons.

First, nobody asked me.

Second, politics bore me.

Third, I have been trying to figure out for years now whether I am a Democrat or a Republican or an Independent, whether I am a Conservative or a Liberal, or even whether I am an Anarchist.

Then there are complications.

For instance, I have never been able to figure out how the tax rate is computed.

Now, I know this has not bothered some mayors who have sat in the front office of City Hall, but it would bother me. Here in Fitchburg the tax rate goes up $1 every time $250,000 more is spent. I'm afraid that it would be impossible for me to keep track of all those quarter-million-dollar expenditures.

You see, I have to look in my wallet to find out how much money I am carrying on my person at any particular moment.

I seldom write a check without making a mistake, usually with my signature.

Balance a checking account? I don't even make an attempt but let the wiser half of our household combination do the honors.

Another thing about being mayor is that you have to make speeches.

And hold press conferences.

And make wise and witty remarks.

That's where I'd be a flop. For instance, how can anyone top Mayor Hedley Bray's comment when the snow rampaged down on the city: "The good Lord brought it and the good Lord will take it away."

Who could ever top that statement as the epitome of something or other?

As far as my political platform goes, it would be thrown out as soon as declared.

Why?

Here's why:

I would order the School Committee to reduce all classrooms to three subjects: reading, writing, and arithmetic. I would ask teachers simply to teach kids to read, teach them to write, and teach them to add, subtract, multiply, and divide. That's it. Nothing else for the first five years of school.

In the sixth grade, one more course would be added: art, perhaps. In the seventh, nature, etc.

You see? No chance at all.

As for running the city:

My motto would be Keep it simple. Which would immediately doom my chances in this world of red tape, multiple copies, bureaucratic jargon, and let's-have-a-study-made.

Whenever a snowstorm hit, there would be No Work as well as No School. Everybody would stay home while the plows cleaned up the stuff.

I would order this because most people hate to drive in the snow. Letting everybody stay home would eliminate traffic jams, skidding accidents, falls on sidewalks, firecracker tempers, and getting mad at the mayor.

This kind of action could lead to impeachment, of course.

So would my order to eliminate all traffic lights.

And to make all streets one-way, as a method of reducing the chances of accidents. It may take you longer to get there but at least you'd eventually arrive.

The library would remain open twenty-four hours a day, seven days a week.

And City Hall would open only one day a week. Thus City Hall would have only eight hours a week to come up with ways to aggravate people.

The workers at City Hall would be transferred to the library.

And then I'd . . .

But enough of this madness.

September 2, 1977

Wearing Those Glasses

MY PROBLEM, DOCTOR, IS THAT I AM ALWAYS OUT OF STEP AND OUT OF STYLE, having been born a generation too late—or too early, maybe.

I mean, all the standards have been changed and I find myself continually bewildered by myself and my place in this strange world of ours.

For instance:

I picked up the paper the other day and read that one of the big fashion trends is people wearing glasses who don't need to wear them.

They wear glasses despite their 20/20 vision, because glasses are now considered in and chic and all that stuff.

This is what I mean about emerging into this world at the wrong time. When I was a kid in the seventh or eighth grade, it got difficult for me to read the blackboard, and the inevitable eye exam revealed that I needed glasses.

That was a sentence of doom to a boy just entering those tender and tentative teenage years.

The glasses were as far from chic as they possibly could be. They perched precariously on the nose. Steel frames, round lenses. An obvious invitation for your classmates to yell: Hey, four-eyes.

Girls were worse off.

Dorothy Parker summed up the terrible situation for girls in that immortal verse:

> Men seldom make passes
> At girls who wear glasses.

Anyway, there I was, viewing the world through heavy spectacles. They'd fall to the ground when I tried some boyish maneuver like jumping over a fence, and then I'd walk around with a cracked lens for a couple of days, keeping my face averted from my mother and father so they wouldn't see the damage.

Finally I decided on an instant cure.

First of all, I "lost" the glasses. We looked everywhere at home, at school, on the well-worn path between home and school. Too bad, but good-bye glasses.

But how will you see? people asked.

I think the eye exam was wrong, I said. I can see just fine. Or maybe my eyesight just came back.

Of course this demanded a certain amount of fakery on my part. And it meant working harder, too. I had to pretend to read what was on the blackboard and had to work feverishly at school to compensate for what I couldn't see.

I managed to hold off parents, teachers, friends, and relatives for a few blissful months of being blind but lensless. I had to capitulate, however, when I failed to recognize my own father waving to me from across the street.

So there I was again. Wearing glasses.

There had been a new development in the optical world. Now the big thing was rimless glasses. I think the psychology of rimless glasses was that they were supposed to be sort of invisible. If people glanced at you quickly, they'd think you weren't wearing glasses at all.

Also, if you kept your head tilted, people might think you looked like Franklin Delano Roosevelt.

Now, the terrible thing about wearing glasses in those days is that the movies—which were probably the biggest social influence we had —always portrayed people who wore glasses as either weaklings or— and this is a word you seldom hear anymore—homely.

Take that girl who worked as a secretary or a store clerk or a bank teller. She wore glasses. She'd meet the handsome leading man in one of those double-feature movies and he wouldn't notice her because she was so, gulp, homely. But there came a time when the glasses would come off and, lo and behold, she was really beautiful. As soon as the glasses vanished she'd shake her head and these beautiful tresses would leap to life, a gorgeous waterfall of hair, and she even looked sexier, too. No wonder no girl wanted to wear glasses.

As for the fellows, look at Clark Kent. Or all those ninety-eight-pound weaklings. Most of them wore glasses so that people would know immediately that they were timid and shy and—weak. Before Clark Kent became Superman, he had to step into a phone booth and remove his glasses.

I didn't aspire to become Superman. I was ready to play the second lead—the guy who probably didn't get the girl but provided a laugh or two—as long as I could divest myself of the glasses.

Now, all these years later, glasses have become chic and the thing to wear. Famous designers fashion new styles. A lot of people have glasses but don't seem ever to wear them. They push them up into their hair, casually. They hold them in their hand and swing them now and then, using them as props to make a point. They have glasses for different days of the week.

Meanwhile, I go along with my bifocals and the memories of those four-eyed years, and my consolation is that I may have provided a laugh or two but I did manage to get the girl in the end.

June 2, 1977

Our Food: Too Fast, Too Much

EAT, DRINK, AND BE MERRY FOR TOMORROW YOU DIET. I DUNNO. EVERYBODY seems to be overweight and anxious about what the scales say. Diet books sell in the millions, especially those that promise you can lose weight and still keep on eating.

Food prices are so high that ceilings are established and boycotts are called. And still we eat. Too much. And too fast.

Now, I'm not going to hand out that "while people are starving elsewhere" business, although it's true. And maybe I'm not the proper person to be writing about food because I am a small eater— by that, I mean I eat small portions—and I am a slow eater. But I find myself in a world of big eaters and fast eaters.

Take, for instance, our restaurants. Most of them are geared to give you plenty of food and to serve it fast. Frankly, I don't want fast service. Let it be moderate. Let me savor the food.

The other night we had dinner at a fine restaurant. But the waitress was out to set some kind of record for speedy service—and the chef apparently believed that good means big.

Probably I got off on the wrong foot because I decided to have a cup of clam chowder with a martini to follow. Apparently this upsets some kind of unwritten rule of restaurants.

"You mean you want the chowder first and the martini afterward?"

"Right," I said.

She looked doubtful, as if saying to herself: I've got a beaut here. But she went her way and was back in a minute with the chowder. And the small bag of crackers. The chowder was delicious. Hot. I sipped it slowly. Beautiful.

Then came the martini. She set the martini down on the table and her hand shot out and grabbed the chowder cup.

"I'm not finished," I said.

"You're not finished?" Disbelief in her eyes. How could I not be finished? It was only a cup, for heaven's sake, and at least five minutes had passed.

Seeking to establish some kind of normality, she said: "How about salad?"

"There's no rush," I said.

"I know. But what kind of dressing would you like when you're ready?"

"Russian."

Off she went and she was gone long enough to allow me to finish the chowder and sip the martini. I didn't bother with the olive.

The salad arrived. I looked at it aghast. The bowl was as big as a hubcap. A lake of Russian dressing was surrounded by a shore of lettuce. I took a few bites. Delicious. A few more bites and I set it aside.

The waitress had evidently been observing our table. She approached us.

"You didn't like the salad," she said.

"It was delicious," I reassured her.

"But you set it aside."

"I know."

Overcome with curiosity now, she said: "Is that all you're going to eat of it?"

"I'm not a big eater," I said.

Frowning, she went her way but not before taking our order for the main dish. My entree consisted of chunks of beef. It has a fancy name but actually it boiled down to chunks of beef.

It seemed as if she had only just departed when she returned. She set down my plate with a triumphant flourish. I regarded the dish with dismay. There must have been, oh, at least fifteen chunks of meat. I figured I could eat maybe five of them.

I began to chew. The food was very good but I could feel pressure building up. I had a feeling she was lurking somewhere in the shadows. The baked potato was also great. But it resembled Rollstone Boulder and I knew I was in for more trouble. I ate six chunks of beef. And sat back.

"You didn't like the beef," she said accusingly.

"I loved it."

"But look at what you've left." She had now adopted a maternal air, an attitude of concern.

"Like I said, I'm a small eater."

"You sure are," she said, accepting the situation finally. But she had something up her sleeve: dessert.

"Let me get you the dessert menu."

"I don't want any," I said.

"You don't want any dessert?"

"That's right. Maybe if you had a small piece of cheddar cheese or a slice of apple."

"We've got all kinds of pie," she said. And began to list them . . .

You get the idea. The trouble is that cooks and chefs and even wives and mothers and mothers-in-law all feel that the meal is a failure unless you clean your plate.

I could clean my plate if they didn't fill it up so much. And the dessert is always something like pecan pie with whipped cream. Or strawberry shortcake.

The dessert arrives and I pale.

"What's the matter? Don't you like my pecan pie?" she asks.

"I love it. I love it. I'm just full, that's all."

But that word "full" is not allowed. There's a terrible ring to it, as far as cooks are concerned.

I have always wished that restaurants had a separate menu for people who don't have big appetites. Children have their own menus—why not small eaters?

The other night I ordered a children's portion of spaghetti, and pizza for the rest of the family. The waiter, of course, placed the small plate of spaghetti in front of our five-and-a-half-year-old. When he had gone, I switched plates.

But I kept looking over my shoulder as I ate. I had a feeling the waiter was going to tap me on the shoulder and order me from the place or something.

Anyway, anyway. If the old saying is right that you are what you eat, then apparently I will never amount to much.

Pass the chowder. Make it a cup, not a bowl.

April 3, 1972

The Big Noise

THERE'S THIS PLACE I HEARD ABOUT WHERE THEY HAVE A JUKEBOX, AND THE great thing about this jukebox is that you can put in a dime and press Number 7 and get three minutes of silence.

Beautiful.

I think that's what the world needs, a little silence around here. Or, at the very least, a little tenderness, some gentleness. Whisper sweet nothings to me, sweetheart. Don't raise your voice to me, buddy.

The noise in our world is getting ridiculous. Not only the car horns and motorcycles and police sirens and jackhammers but a lot of other oral junk as well.

Television commercials, for instance.

The stations deny it, but it seems to me that they turn up the volume during commercials. What happens is that you start watching a half-hour show in pleasant fashion but by the time the last credits are given, everybody is screaming at you from the tube.

But that's only one minor instance.

Most of the time we bring it on ourselves. For instance, any house with teenagers may have a television and a stereo going at the same time, with punctuation marks provided by the telephone. And all of this is accomplished with the volume on high.

While outside, if it's a window-opener day, they're tearing up the street again.

And a helicopter whirls overhead.

The worst part of it all is that, most of the time, we don't really notice all the noise.

In fact, an article in a recent *New York Times* says that noise has become so pervasive in our lives that we no longer "hear" it.

The decibels are going up.

And the chances of deafness are also going up.

This article also explained what decibels are exactly—I've always had only a vague idea. Well, a decibel is a measure of sound energy. One decibel is the smallest change in sound that the human ear can detect. The leaves rustle at 12 decibels. Ordinary conversation is carried on at 45 to 50 decibels. Most office noise is at 65 decibels. The danger points begin somewhere around 75 or 80 decibels. And the leap from 80 to 90 is deceptive—it's not really just 10 decibels, because the ear perceives it as twice as much noise. Snowmobiles are 115 DECIBELS.

Deafness isn't the only threat here.

Experts say that noise causes fatigue, weight loss, ulcers, and high blood pressure. It's been a factor in nervous breakdowns. And it's affected the learning ability of children.

Of course, one person's noise may be sweet delight to another person.

There's this man who's a writer, see. Or at least he makes his living at the typewriter. But he finds it hard to write in perfect silence. It gets on his nerves. At the office, there're the familiar sounds of the teletype and the other typewriters and the telephones. One reason he clings to an old battered typewriter is that it makes a beautiful staccato sound as the keys hit the paper.

In the room at home which he laughingly calls his den, he usually types to the sound of music on the stereo. Nothing heavy—a current pop tune.

"Feelings," for instance, which he places on the turntable as he puts the stereo on automatic.

The words march onto the paper as the music plays. Minutes pass, and then an hour or two. Until someone finally says:

"If I hear that song one more time, I'll scream."

So he changes the record to an old standby—something by Neil Diamond, maybe. And he's all set for another hour or two.

Funny thing about noise.

We create it ourselves. And hate to give it up.

That same story in the *Times* says that some noises can be reduced but people resist it. There's a belief that noise is synonymous with power.

What happened was this: A company produced a vacuum cleaner that made almost no noise at all. When it was test-marketed, the machine hardly sold. So the company did more testing to find out the reason for the sales resistance. They learned that people felt the cleaner wasn't doing a good job. Too quiet.

Anyway, anyway.

The absence of sound is also a kind of noise. They tell of the man who lived in an apartment with thin walls near a factory that produced weapons during World War II. The motors throbbed in the factory twenty-four hours a day, never stopping.

When word was flashed that the war was over, the factory owners halted all the machinery to mark the moment.

The sleeping man next door woke up with a start.

"What was that?" he asked in the sudden silence.

December 11, 1975

The Gum Caper

SO THERE I WAS IN THAT SMALL VARIETY STORE IN THE UPPER COMMON, standing in line with the junior high school kids from B. F. Brown, waiting to pay for, of all things, bubble gum.

I'll say one thing about the kids—they didn't regard me with either suspicion or hostility or amusement. They simply assumed that this bewildered-looking adult liked bubble gum and was being very careful about picking out the right kind. But it so happens that I have not chewed gum in years and the reason I was buying some was . . .

But let's go back a bit.

A minor accident a couple of days before had left the car crippled by a radiator with two leaks. The problem was getting the car to that garage out of town where it could receive the attention of Wally, the foreman.

Wally is a terrific mechanic. More than that: he is a true craftsman, almost an artist at his work. He takes pride in the jobs he performs. He treats cars and motors with reverence.

Anyway, I called Wally about the accident and about the radiator and asked him if he could send a tow truck up this way to haul the car in. Wally said he would have to hire an outside tow truck. Then he added: "But you can drive it down here yourself."

"But the radiator has two leaks and won't hold the water," I said.

"What you do is this—get some chewing gum and seal up the leaks," Wally said.

Now, if I didn't know that Wally was an expert, I'd have ignored the suggestion and said, "Just send the tow truck."

I mean: chewing gum, for crying out loud.

But I trust Wally implicitly in matters mechanical, and although I was still doubtful, I went up to the store and bought the gum. It took me a while to buy it because I was looking for volume—and I finally figured that bubble gum would do the trick.

Back home, I asked a certain child, who has just turned seven, if she felt like chewing some gum. "Bubble gum," I said.

She greeted the question with surprise because ordinarily we don't encourage her to chew gum. In fact, we discourage her.

I said: "I've got a couple of packages here that have to be chewed right away."

Her eyes danced with delight, all disbelief suspended. "How come, Dad?" she asked.

"Well, the radiator in the car leaks and I'm going to use the gum to plug up the holes."

"Oh," she said, accepting the answer without question. She has complete faith in her father, despite the cut fingers and scratched hands my projects usually inflict upon me. She goes right on believing.

So we sat there chewing awhile and it was fun, in a way. We blew a couple of bubbles because, after all, that's what bubble gum is all about. And then we went out to challenge the car.

I lifted the hood, unscrewed the radiator cap (which took a few minutes: I finally had to pry it off) and inserted the hose in the mouth of the radiator.

The faucet was turned on and the water gushed into the radiator— and, sure enough, the water spurted from the leaks.

I had hoped, really, that the radiator might have sealed itself or something, because, frankly, I didn't think the gum would work. And I could envision myself on a back road somewhere with a radiator suddenly turning into a fountain as the gum gave way.

Despite the doubts, I took the chewing gum and jammed it against the leaks and the spurting stopped. I refilled the radiator and looked again. No leaks.

Later, we went off to the garage and the trip passed without incident. In fact, it was beautiful. Near Fort Devens, a plane flew low overhead and nine or ten parachutists tumbled out and they floated in the air like blossoms falling from a tree. That was worth the trip alone.

At the garage, I handed Wally the keys and said, in triumph, "I made it."

He didn't seem the least bit surprised.

"Thanks, Wally," I said. And as I left the place I looked at all that sophisticated equipment, the lifts and the fancy tools and stuff. And I shook my head.

I think there's a moral here somewhere. Maybe it's got something to do with the simple approach to life, how we often become so caught up in our vaunted technology that we overlook the small, commonsense solutions to our problems.

The funny thing is that it takes a true expert to know when technology is required and when a simple touch is needed. Wally is that kind of expert.

Incidentally, the gum tasted very good.

May 23, 1974

The Whatchamacallits Are Taking Over the World

I HAVE JUST RETURNED FROM THE BACKYARD, WHERE THE POWER LAWN mower perished—there was a sudden strident sound as the blade accelerated, a small explosion like a Fourth of July firecracker going off, and then silence. I pulled the cord in an effort to start the mower but the cord was limp in my hand. A neighbor who knows all about these things advised me: "The thing is dead. It'll never mow again."

My first response was a kind of relief because I didn't feel like mowing the lawn in the first place, and the mower quit before I'd finished two rows of the backyard. Then dismay set in: the prospect of buying a new mower. Then more dismay: a kind of despair considering the state of gadgetry in the house today.

I own a stereo phonograph that can't play a record without skipping here and there on the disc, making Tony Bennett sound like some kind of demented street singer.

The tape recorder refuses to record.

The wind raised havoc with the television antenna a while back and a new antenna was purchased. The installers of the antenna assured us it would bring in both UHF and VHF programs, but they lied of course. The VHF channels are fuzzy and snowy—and these are the channels on which the baseball games appear, and baseball games are about all that seem worth watching on television these days.

Two weeks ago, in the middle of important work that meant overtime at the typewriter, the typewriter broke down. The whatchamacallit didn't work anymore. The typewriter repairman is on vacation, but his secretary let me borrow another machine for the moment. But a new typewriter to a person who earns his daily bread at the keyboard presents a traumatic experience. I am like a carpenter without his favorite saw or a chef without his favorite pan.

Lawn mower dead, tape recorder silent, stereo hiccuping, to say nothing of the furnace, which showed signs of collapse a month or so ago, necessitating a repair job equal to a week's pay and the cheerful comment of the repairman: "You're lucky—at least it didn't conk out in the middle of January."

We have, of course, become slaves to our gadgets and our appliances and all our luxuries. In fact, our luxuries are no longer luxuries, and that's what panics us when they fail to work. The car is now a necessity. When it's in the garage for one of the thousand "small repair jobs" a car is heir to, a state of emergency exists. If you see a man walking around dazed and disoriented, you know instantly that his car is in the garage.

Toys were once simply playthings. Now they have become luxuries. You don't push the little truck, it's self-propelled. Toys now require special electrical adaptors, and even battery-powered toys are considered old fashioned. Toys also come with guarantees and warranties. The day will probably arrive when schools will carry such courses as "Care and Repair of Christmas Toys" or "Automatic Versus Manual Toy Machinery."

The problem is that our seduction by the gadgets has been deceptive. And gradual. There was a time when I was content to ride a secondhand bike, with balloon tires and no fenders. It was sheer bliss to speed along Spruce Street even in the rain and get soaked as I cruised through puddles. But now my children require bikes with ten speeds and odometers and we take them in for ninety-day checkups.

Once I was content to drive a battered Plymouth with a manual floor shift that called upon muscles I didn't know I possessed. Now I am contemplating the possibility of a car with air-conditioning, to say nothing of stereo cassettes to fill the frigid air with music. And I do this knowing that inevitably the air-conditioning unit will break down and the stereo cassette will fail to dispense its music, and I will be fuming and fussing as I drive along in the heat and the silence.

The thing about our gadgets is that they leave us helpless when they don't work anymore. As a boy I used to earn summer spending-money by pushing a hand-powered lawn mower at homes in the old neighborhood. The mower was simple and beautiful. I never remember having it break down. I was in control at all times even though I huffed and puffed a bit.

But the power lawn mower is different. We are in its power. When the mower simply stopped working this morning, so did I. I could only look down at it. I could have pushed it all over the lawn and nothing would have happened. It has always been temperamental anyway, refusing to start, for instance, unless I adjust certain levers to certain positions and place my foot in the proper spot as I pull the starting cord. Any deviation kept the motor mute and defiant. When it quit altogether this morning, I could have sworn the mower issued a small cackle of delight just before it expired.

Is it paranoia to think this? Perhaps. But let me submit the following as evidence that something strange is happening in this gadgetry land of ours.

A plant in our vicinity recently remodeled some of its factory space to install air-conditioning units. But air-conditioning was not provided on all four floors of the building, only in two sections of the factory. There's a reason for this, of course. Air-conditioning was installed in one section where a computer compiles payrolls and other statistical data. And it was also installed in another area where a computer is involved with production. The computers require air-conditioning. Or, as they say these days, a controlled environment. Yet the workers must do their jobs in the old-fashioned heat of summer and the drafts of winter (it's an ancient building).

I ponder things like that as I sit at this unfamiliar typewriter, which has a personality of its own, and adjust to it. (Notice that the machine does not have to adjust to me.) I wonder when the whatchamacallit will give out again.

From where I sit, I could look up and see my expired lawn mower in the backyard. But I'm not going to look. I am afraid that it is wearing a look of triumph as it joins thousands of other mowers and gadgets that quit working throughout the land this morning.

The whatchamacallits are taking over the world.

September 1978

A Brush with Two Goliaths

I HAD A BRUSH WITH TWO OF THE GOLIATHS OF OUR WORLD LAST WEEK—THE post office and Detroit—and, frankly, I felt like David without a slingshot.

And I also felt as though I had stumbled into the pages of *Catch-22*.

It began when I arrived home and found, among other mail, a card indicating that there was an "article" awaiting me at the post office. An attempt apparently had been made to deliver the piece of mail but to no avail.

I called the post office to learn what it was all about. According to the notice, the article was "certified" mail, which made it sound important enough to check on right away, as far as I was concerned.

And thus began this strange phone call with the *Catch-22* overtones.

I told the fellow who answered the phone what had happened and asked if he could give me any information. Fine. First, I told him I was puzzled because the certified article hadn't been delivered.

"Was anybody home?" he asked.

"Yes, all day long."

"Does your doorbell work?"

Well, that's where he had me. One of the peculiarities of our house, which incidentally endears it to me, is that we really have two front doors, separated only by three steps and probably five feet or so. The door to the left contains the mail slot where the mail is ordinarily deposited. The doorbell there doesn't ring.

"There's your answer," he said. "Your doorbell doesn't ring and he figured nobody was home."

"But it hasn't worked for years," I said. "I thought he might have tried the other front door." I know this is unreasonable of me.

"We are allowed only one entry to a house," he said.

I said: "What?"

"We are allowed only one entry to a house. The entry with the mail slot is the official entry. It would have been illegal for him to go to the other door."

"Illegal to try another door?"

"Right," he said.

"Well, how about when postage is due on a letter?" I asked. "The mailman always comes to the other door."

"That's illegal," he said.

"But he takes the money and leaves the letter," I said.

"It's still illegal—only one entry to a house."

I am always confounded by situations like this, although I admit that I should have that doorbell fixed. I then remembered that our regular mailman was on vacation and, of course, that's why the substitute hadn't come to the other door.

"Look," I said, "the notice says that I can reschedule the article to be delivered tomorrow. Can I do that?"

"Yes," he said.

"Which door will he come to?"

"The door with the mail slot. That's the official entry to the house."

"Suppose I put up a little sign that says: Bell out of order—please use other door?" I've been putting up these little signs for years, but sooner or later they come down.

"The door with the mail slot is the official entry to the house," he said.

This went on for a while. He was very polite. In fact, I knew that he was just doing his job and that phone calls of this nature must turn his days into a mild sort of hell.

But frankly, the conversation was beginning to fascinate me. There was a certain rhythm and style to the questions and answers that could have been put to music.

And the thought also occurred that he was putting me on.

"Listen," I said, "could you give me an idea of what the article is?"

Apparently this wasn't illegal. He asked: "Where is it from?"

"Detroit."

"That sounds like a recall," he said.

"What's recall?"

"Your car. It sounds like it's being recalled." Beautiful. I was about to get out of the clutches of the post office only to become involved in the toils of Detroit.

Anyway, anyway. We hung up on good terms, and despite the illegality of the situation, I made a little sign for the out-of-order doorbell and sure enough the next day the mailman came to the other front door and left the "certified article."

It was a letter all right. It opened: "Dear Customer." Nothing like the personal touch. And it went on:

"Your vehicle is equipped with a six-cylinder engine having a fuel pump which may possibly develop a fuel leakage condition. If fuel leakage were to occur, the leaking fuel could ignite, resulting in an engine compartment fire."

It went into a lot of details and suggested that I get in touch with the dealer, of course. It was nice to know they wouldn't charge me for the replacement if needed. But they said nothing about compensation for the lost time and the threat of hazard. And those words kept recurring to me: "the leaking fuel could ignite, resulting in an engine compartment fire."

The letter closed, touchingly:

"We sincerely regret the necessity of this action and any inconvenience which it may cause you, but we are certain you understand our interest in your continued satisfaction with your vehicle."

What continued satisfaction? The front door on the passenger side won't open from the inside, although the dealer has already worked on it. The safety belt alarm system is also getting on my nerves.

So I went to the telephone and called the dealer.

But that's another story.

February 27, 1973

A Few Rules for Survival

TO GET ALONG IN THIS OFTEN BEWILDERING WORLD OF OURS, YOU HAVE TO use all the ingenuity at your command. Sometimes you have to play games. Or not let your right hand know what your left foot is doing.

As the years go by and youth flees—a lovely leaf hustled away by an errant wind—you have to resort to tricks. Or emergency aid. For instance, I find that I have to write notes to myself all the time even though half the time I don't know what they mean when I run across them later.

You also pick up a bit of wisdom now and then. This means learning not to make the same mistake more than five or six times.

You learn to use whatever weapons are in your meager arsenal. For example, a long time ago I learned the value of addition and subtraction, although I was terrible in math at school.

But this is a special kind of arithmetic and it goes like this:

Whenever she says she's going downtown to shop and will be back in an hour, I always add at least a half hour to the time she says she'll return. And maybe even more than that, depending on how many errands she has on her list.

The same principle applies to repairmen. If the mechanic at the garage says the repair job will take twenty minutes, I figure it will be forty-five minutes. And if he says the car will be ready at two o'clock, I automatically make it three o'clock.

This saves a lot of frustration and disappointment.

This addition and subtraction can be used in many ways. If a movie is hailed as terrific, I figure that it will be very good. And if someone says the movie was pretty good, I expect it to be just fair.

(There are other variations. When I was a regular reader of *Time* magazine, I learned that if *Time* panned a movie, I would probably like it. And if they praised the film, I'd always be sure to avoid it. The same applies to the front page review of the *New York Times Book Review*. Nine out of ten times, the book reviewed in that spot is a bore. To me at least.)

Another thing: If there's a new series on television that everybody's raving about and I decide to try it, I know that the night I watch the series it will be one of the weaker stories. You should have seen last week's, someone always says.

The object of all these subterfuges is not to be eternally pessimistic but to leave yourself wide open for some surprises. Because that's just what happens. Life becomes a series of small but sweet happenings. Sometimes the movie turns out to be terrific, after all.

There are all sorts of things an inhabitant of this planet needs to use to wend his way through the nights and days with the least amount of trouble.

I have found that the word "quite" is absolutely indispensable. What crises this word has avoided, what friendships it has preserved.

For instance, someone shows you the latest picture of his baby. And you look at it and say: "That's quite a baby."

Notice, now, that you haven't said that it's a beautiful baby or that it resembles every other nine-month-old in the world. But the word "quite" takes care of it.

(Actually, I picked up the use of the word years ago when I showed a picture of our most recent baby to a friend and realized that he had used the word "quite" several times but had said little else. I can't understand it, either, because the baby, I thought, was really beautiful.)

Anyway, anyway. You can use "quite" to slip out of a lot of tight corners.

"Say, that's quite a tie all right."

"That was quite a book."

"Hey, that's quite a pair of shoes."

Endless, really.

The idea, of course, is to be kind, not cruel. And "quite" should never be used in jest or to avoid giving a compliment. You should, in fact, practice the use of "quite," pronouncing it carefully so that you don't show false enthusiasm and yet don't allow any sarcasm to leak out. It's quite an art, really.

So there you have it, a few rules for surviving with a minimum of fuss in this turbulent world.

They make quite a column, don't they?

December 6, 1973

The Invitation Says R.S.V.P.

I HAVE THIS THING ABOUT PARTIES. I'M NOT TALKING ABOUT OFFICE PARTIES at holiday time or gatherings with old friends or neighbors. I mean the kind of party where the invitation arrives by mail. R.S.V.P. Beautiful: to be wanted by somebody. Our presence is desired. Isn't that what we all wish for? To be wanted?

But then, all these doubts. First of all, I'm never certain when we should arrive. On time? But suppose we're the first ones to ring the doorbell—doesn't that make us seem too eager, as if we haven't been to a party in ages and can't wait for the festivities to begin? On the other hand, why keep kind people waiting? Why play these deadly social games that I detest? And, of course, arriving too late would mean missing some of the evening. So we compromise, choosing a time that doesn't seem too early or too late. But I've never found out, really, what the proper time is.

The next problem is: Who's going to be there? I don't ask this in a snobbish sense but simply because it's unsettling to walk into a roomful or a houseful of virtual strangers. The identity of your hosts provides a clue to the others, of course. But not always. It depends. Anyway, there's really no way of finding out who else is going. You have a feeling that a certain couple also has been invited. But it's impossible to ask them. Because—suppose they haven't been asked, after all? And they're probably wondering if you're going and also hesitate to ask.

Then the arrival. Two kinds, really. One: you enter the house and are confronted by that roomful of strangers. Your impulse is to flee. Or are you in the wrong house? Did they mean the invitation for someone else? You stand there for a small eternity with a terrible smile on your face. Then your hostess rushes forward. Charming and gracious. She pulls you both into the house in a grand gesture. "So happy you could come." Stuff to do with hats and coats. The heart warms.

The other kind of arrival is where you enter the house and know most of the people. A gathering of acquaintances, friends among them. The relief that follows is as refreshing as the punch you will be sipping in a few moments. Speaking of punch, there's always a problem of what to drink at parties. I am a man of simple tastes—a bottle of beer is companion enough. But who wants to stroll through a party juggling a bottle or can of beer? And so I improvise and ultimately find my way to the punch bowl. Warm sherry with apples, perhaps. Or punch laced with champagne.

And now the conversation. I always envy these people who can carry on casual conversations without effort or seeming effort, their words dancing brightly, like pebbles skimming across the surface of a pond. They wander from group to group, always holding someone's interest. I stand there, thinking of possible topics. I remember those ads for certain magazines that say: Be an interesting conversationalist. Now I wished I'd subscribed. I also envy these men who hold a glass in one hand, a cigarette in another, looking dashing and debonair. In fact, they seem to have a third hand available to light ladies' cigarettes or shake other people's hands.

Then, suddenly, the magic happens. Perhaps it's the punch or the aura of a party when everything is going well. Suddenly all the people are charming and endowed with grace. There's a kind of mutual affection that swells and moves through the rooms, embracing everyone. There may be actual music playing, but there's also the music of voices, a lilting litany that sings of a happy time. And suddenly I myself am dashing and debonair and almost wish I smoked again so I could flourish that cigarette. I murmur a remark and it sounds witty, amusing. As the evening glides on, you hate to see the party end. But it must, of course. Calls of "good night" linger on the air.

Catching sight of myself in the mirror when we arrive at home, I realize that I am not, after all, dashing and debonair. I knew all the time it was an illusion, anyway. But if a party can, for a few moments, nourish you with that kind of sweet illusion, wasn't it worthwhile going for that alone, to say nothing of all the other pleasures?

January 14, 1971

Color Me Green

IF ENVY WERE A VIRTUE, THEN I WOULD BE THE MOST VIRTUOUS MAN WALKING the earth, although perhaps it's not exactly envy that assails me constantly. However, that's the nearest word that applies. Certainly there is admiration in the envy, and wistfulness as well and not a little bit of jealousy. Anyway, for want of a more precise word, I employ envy.

For instance, I am envious of the fellow who always catches the waiter's eye immediately. But more than that. He rattles off what he wishes to be served after merely glancing at one of those intimidating menus in a fancy restaurant where even the bus boy acts as if he has a chauffeured limousine waiting outside. And I envy the fellow who always knows precisely how much and whom to tip.

I break out in unabashed envy at the fellow whose handshake is always hearty and crunching, and whose palms never moisten as he waits to be introduced to an important person.

And there's envy of the fellow who sits in the dentist's chair and says, "Never mind the novocaine—go ahead and drill."

And the fellow whose desk never seems to get cluttered. Or the fellow who never spills coffee or glue pots and can eat a jelly doughnut without requiring a napkin.

There are many people who cause my inhibitions to pile up inside. I am inhibited by the fellow who never sits behind a nine-foot giant or a lady with a big hat in the theater, and the fellow who always stands in the line that moves at the bank or the supermarket or the box office, and the fellow who calls up at the last minute and manages to get the choicest seats in the house.

How can I help but feel jealousy toward the fellow whose car breaks down and who jumps out, lifts the hood, tinkers with something inside, and then gets back in and drives away. When my car grinds to a halt, I lift the hood because that seems the proper thing to do, but the inside of the car looks exactly like what it is: the inside of a car.

I am eloquent with envy of the fellow who knows exactly what to say standing next to a pretty girl at the bus stop or in a theater lobby. Or who always makes those clever remarks after being introduced at a cocktail party. The most dazzling and sophisticated remarks leap to my lips, but that only happens when I'm driving home.

As a boy, I was emerald with envy of the kid whose pencil never broke during a test, who never tore his trousers scaling a fence, and who was never chased by a bully. And there was the poignant envy of the kid who always was asked to dance when the "Girls' Choice" was announced. How I stood there with racing heart as the lovely girl approached and then plunged into envy when she asked that other fellow to dance.

So many people to envy or admire. The fellow who finished his cellar into a paneled recreation room or the guy who repairs his own faucets or the man who practically adds a new wing to his house, for crying out loud, while I have difficulty finding the right grooves when changing a light bulb.

Envy? It leaps all over the place when I consider the fellow who never forgets, who always knows who he's calling on the telephone, for instance. I get terribly embarrassed when I dial the number, someone answers, and I find to my horror that I've forgotten who I'm calling. And speaking of numbers, I have admiration for those fellows who remember zip codes and car number plates and social security numbers. Or who keep their desk calendars up to date.

Anyway, anyway.

We are envious of others but must cherish what we possess. Thus I am envious of the fellow whose face leaps out at mine while I'm shaving, particularly when I have just looked into the bedroom, seen the shining child there curled around a teddy bear, touched the soft hair of her head, and heard her murmur: "Don't work too hard today, dear old dad."

And it doesn't seem to matter, after all, that the other fellow always was asked to dance when the "Girls' Choice" came along.

March 12, 1970

The Game of Us and Them

THE WORLD IS MADE UP OF TWO KINDS OF PEOPLE—THEM AND US. OH, I'M not talking about friends versus enemies or the Western nations against the rest of the world or the North against the South. Nothing like that. I mean those of us who share common things, who are loyal to each other, and those who aren't. And with people who are with Us, we have special rules and very special ways of looking at Them and Us.

For instance:

We are always Cautious but they are Chicken.

When we lose a football game by a 7 to 6 score, we achieve a Moral Victory. But when they lose a football game to us by a 7 to 6 score, we say that it's the score that counts.

When we don't dress, we go Casual. But when they don't dress, they're Slobs.

Our house has character—theirs is rundown. Or our house has that lived-in look—their house looks worn out.

A friend of ours is colorful, but that same friend of theirs is nutty.

Our friend has an even disposition and never loses his cool—their friend is dull, dull, dull.

Our friend is the life of the party—but their friend always makes a fool of himself after a few drinks.

See how it works?

Our garden could have used more luck this year—their garden was an utter failure.

Or: We have a green thumb—but they happen to have good soil.

We are slender—but they are skinny.

We have been putting on a little weight lately, but they are getting fat.

We are contemplative—they are lazy.

We are daredevils—they are reckless.

The Them or Us syndrome extends to the arts, as well.

As in:

Our friend got a character part in a new movie—their friend got a small role.

Our friend has written a book with a plot as light as a soufflé—their friend has written a book with a flimsy plot.

Our friend is very emotional—their friend is temperamental.

Our friend is always "on"—their friend is a show-off.

Our friend is multi-talented—their friend can sing a little, dance a little, play a little.

The world of diplomacy has also been invaded by this kind of thing and, in fact, it has reached the stage where the magazine *Horizon* devotes an article to what it calls "Newspeak." Samples:

They have terrorists—we have freedom fighters.

They are moralistic—we are moral.

They are reactionary—we are traditional.

They are racist—we want to preserve our identity.

They have emotions—we have feelings.

But most of all, it is used in our daily lives, and it goes unnoticed.

Our friend is fastidious—their friend is fussy.

Our friend hasn't been feeling well for some time—their friend is a hypochondriac.

Our children are inquisitive—their children are nosy.

Our friend is very well informed—their friend is a know-it-all.

Our friend can go on at length on any topic—their friend never stops talking.

Our friend is aging gracefully—their friend is getting old.
Ah, but you get the idea. Because you, my friend, are so percep-
tive . . .

September 29, 1976

The Invisible Man Who Follows Me

THERE'S THIS INVISIBLE MAN WHO FOLLOWS ME AROUND. OR MAYBE HE'S NOT
invisible at all. Maybe he's there all right, and can be seen, but I never
see him because I don't turn around fast enough. Either that, or he's
one step ahead of—or behind—me. Anyway, this interloper is a mer-
chant of mischief whose single intent it to give me moments of irrita-
tion and annoyance. Nothing world-shaking but the kind of small
slivers of harassment that make you aware of your shortcomings.

For instance, this thing about paintings. There is always a picture
to hang simply because I am surrounded by painters in this house of
mine—and one particular nineteen-year-old artist whose paintings are
all grace and glory. And so I have all the paraphernalia at hand: drills
and special wire and tape measure and the other stuff. Take it from
me, I am very scientific about the entire operation, probably the only
job I approach scientifically. (I was great at arithmetic in school until
we got around to addition, subtraction, and the rest.) So I hang the
picture beautifully. Then I turn my back—and the invisible man
strikes. The picture dangles crookedly on the wall.

You never know when he's going to strike, of course. Say that you
have to make an important telephone call. And the line is busy—and
stays busy. You know who placed the call to tie up the line, don't you?
Right. Or, say that there's a book or record that you want to buy,
immediately. When I'm struck by a song, I am obsessed until I can
make the purchase, take it home, and play it at least fifteen times in
succession. But how many times does the invisible man get there
before me! "Just sold the last one," the clerk says.

The maddening part of the invisible man is that he hides things.
You could have sworn you left the book on the arm of the chair but
you find it tucked under the newspaper. He has fun with the newspa-

per, too, removing the sports page and leaving it in the next room. At night he bangs the shutter in the side window, but only when it's windy and you're reading a horror story and he waits until after midnight. He also keeps turning the faucet on little by little to make it drip. This he reserves until you wake up at three in the morning. "Is he awake?" the invisible man asks. "Quick, the faucet."

Sometimes I think there are a lot of invisible men around. In fact, they probably belong to The Organization. You know The Organization. The one that doesn't let it rain on Friday but waits until Sunday, that allows you to have the perfect martini in your favorite restaurant but sees to it that the meat and vegetables are cold. Allows a dazzling young woman to smile at you on the street until you smile back and realize she meant the smile for someone else. And then she and that someone else stare disapprovingly at you. I don't know. Maybe they belong to the Organization.

Anyway, anyway. There probably are invisible people somewhere or an organization that chuckles at our petty plans, shakes its head at our foibles and frustrations, our displays of pride and pretension, as we struggle with the daily annoyances, standing in the wrong line at the bank, not having a nickel for the parking meter, getting home and finding out the sweater is the wrong size, waiting for the bus that's only late when it's raining. They reduce us to—what? The realization that we are all human, perhaps. And so we try to outwit those who would spoil our brief time on this planet. At least, I keep hanging those pictures. A sunrise caught in hues that sing looks just as beautiful when viewed at an angle.

February 11, 1971

The Queen and I

NO OFFENSE INTENDED, BUT I'M GLAD I'M NOT MARRIED TO ELIZABETH, THE Queen of England.

And if she were aware of my existence, I imagine she would have nothing to do with this commoner.

Actually, at one time, Elizabeth was very appealing. This is when we both were kids and they'd run her picture in the rotogravure section. (When was the last time anybody used the word "rotogra-vure"?) Anyway, they'd run her picture there and she was pretty and glamorous and probably riding a horse or posing prettily in a white dress.

Those were the years of impossible dreams. A boy at a certain age keeps getting involved emotionally with girls and women beyond his reach, beyond any kind of attainability. And this very unattainability is the wine that feeds the love. These loves are also very safe. They allow a boy to daydream while reality waits outside the dock.

Now, I never really had a crush on Elizabeth. I had a crush on a girl who lived on Water Street and I was hopelessly in love with Merle Oberon. The two emotions were very different. And so was the feeling about young Princess Elizabeth. She was exotic and glamorous. She was "Once upon a time" come alive. We followed her comings and goings the way people today follow the many events in the lives of Princess Caroline and the Kennedy offspring.

Age finally intercedes, of course, and changes everything. The winsome Elizabeth suddenly turned middle-aged at twenty-six. She became matronly overnight. And the lost princess never came back.

A recent issue of *Esquire* featured an article about Queen Elizabeth by Jon Bradshaw. It illuminated the woman that sweet child became and it also enumerated the trappings of royalty. Enough to cause shudders.

According to Bradshaw, the royal person is five feet four inches tall, weighs 119 pounds, is known as "The Big Chick" in certain smart London circles, and likes people to stand up straight when they talk to her.

(One is not introduced to Queen Elizabeth, one is presented.)

The queen, Bradshaw reports, speaks in a rather high-pitched voice. Officially, she has no opinions. As a child, she had a habit of jumping out of bed several times each night to check that her clothes were neatly arranged and that her shoes were set in order. She never went to school. She stood during many of her private lessons so that she would grow accustomed to standing for long periods of time without tiring. The subjects she disliked most were geography and math. (This is probably the only thing we had in common.)

The glamorous life of royalty? She has never yawned in public. She is not permitted to vote. She has no passport. She goes shopping once a year. She has no last name. She suffers from sinus trouble. She rarely carries money. She has a staff that waits on the staff.

She has never been known to lose her temper—but she proves her humanity ultimately by often becoming bored watching Prince Charles playing polo in Windsor Park.

It is probably just as well that these public figures remain removed from us, I guess. For instance, movie stars are always shorter than they appear on the screen. Phyllis Battelle wrote about Mary Tyler Moore the other day and reported that she is extremely thin, that she is mainly interested in her work, she doesn't entertain, doesn't raise flowers, doesn't have kids, and there's not a lot for her to do except work. Mary is also learning to play killer tennis.

My Mary? Killer tennis?

And my lovely young Elizabeth, who has grown up to outwalk most men her age, is a stickler for punctuality, whose favorite pastime is the *Daily Telegraph* crossword puzzle? How age changes us. Me, also, of course.

September 9, 1976

The Year I Drove Through the Car Wash . . .

THE PAST YEAR, WHICH IS FAST BECOMING JUST A MEMORY, IS THE YEAR I drove through the car wash at fifty miles an hour. At least, it felt like fifty miles an hour. The car catapulted through the wash cycle, the wax cycle, and the dry cycle at a ridiculous rate of speed, and then aimed for the street at the end of the tunnel as if shot out of a cannon. The water and the wax had not yet dried—the car looked as if it had caught some terrible disease.

Without looking behind, I drove quickly to one of those do-it-yourself car washes, where I put two quarters in the slot to pay for five minutes of water to wash the gunk off. It was not one of my more glorious moments.

What happened was this: I had driven into the car wash for a $2.75 "wash-and-wax" job, and the attendant took the money and then told me to put the car in neutral. Some kind of conveyor belt would carry the car through the various operations.

I had forgotten that my car was a bit temperamental when it came to shifting. Sometimes the shift pops out of gear into neutral when I come to a stop position. I'd been meaning to have it checked, but it didn't happen often enough to rush me to the garage.

Anyway, that day I followed the attendant's instructions and put the gear into neutral from the park position. But somehow the gear slipped into drive, which I did not expect, of course. In fact, at first I thought the forward motion was the conveyor belt, taking both the car and me into the garage.

Then suddenly we picked up speed before the astonished eyes of the attendant. We shot through the tunnel, through all the paraphernalia of the operations—brushes, buffers, and waxers—with what seemed like the speed of sound. At the end of the tunnel we zoomed out into the street while I clutched the steering wheel, relieved to see that no cars were approaching.

"What happened then?" Bobbie asked after I had told my family the story at an evening meal.

"Nothing," I said.

"Didn't you go back to the car wash?"

"Of course not," I replied.

"I don't blame you," Peter said. "They might have arrested you for speeding in a car wash."

We all laughed. It was a nice moment. We were relaxing after the dishes had been taken away, the aroma of coffee filling the air. We had been talking about the past year and, without pausing to think of the possible consequences, I had told them about my experience with the car wash.

The story delighted the children—who are no longer children. Peter and Bobbie are married, in fact, and I realized I had given them ammunition for the future. I could imagine them, years from now, when they gather together and one of them will say, "Remember the time Dad drove through that car wash . . . ?"

Other things happened last year, too, because each year has its quota of events, the good and the bad, the sweet and the sorrowful, the trivial and the terrific. The milestones and the small incidents stand side by side, disparate, perhaps, but making a sweet kind of harmony.

It was the year that Chris, our second daughter, graduated from college, and Renée, who at twelve is the youngest, won first place in the high jump at summer camp. I didn't climb any mountains last year and wasn't received at Buckingham Palace when we visited London. On the other hand, I did not start smoking again and my weight remained the same as the year before without any dieting.

It's impossible, of course, to review a year and to select things that happened in the order of importance. The small events are not always unimportant. A walk in the woods with Renée when we talked about the changing of the seasons and what makes a bird fly and the longing she confessed for growing up and becoming either a veterinarian or a writer or maybe both—that was a vital moment in 1979, although it may not have seemed so as it happened.

Can we contrast this with a trip to Arizona when we drove toward the Mexican border in a rented car, mountains in their grandeur towering in the distance, giving us a sense of how grand our country is?

In a way, I rediscovered America this year, not so much in travels to such different places as Cleveland and Denver and Dallas, but by leaving the country itself. On a narrow street in London just off Piccadilly Circus, I was suddenly assailed for a moment by homesickness, and I looked forward to a walk across the Common in my hometown on my way to the public library.

All things end and so did 1979, the year when for the first time I kept a daily journal. Each night before going to bed, I entered the events of the day on three-by-five index cards.

A while ago, I took out the small stack of cards and read over some of them. I was amazed at the similarity of the day-by-day events: the record of birds coming to the feeders ("2 cardinals, 1 downy woodpecker, 1 nuthatch, the usual sparrows—Sat., Jan. 7"); the trips to the library; the movies, letters, and phone calls; the visits from friends; the weather ("Nice, brisk sunny day but no touch of spring yet in the air—Fri., Apr. 2"); the comings and goings of a wife, daughters, and a son.

It struck me how unremarkable the events of the year seemed to be, aside from the occasional travels and journeys. Yet, this very unremarkableness provides a bit of warmth and comfort when reviewing the year. The turning of the seasons, the repetitions, the dependable routines—birds that always come back, old friends who always drop in—give me a strange sense of security.

And how can a year be counted as routine when I drove through a car wash at fifty miles an hour? At least, it felt like fifty miles an hour.

January 1980

Checking Out My Condition

LIKE THE SONG SAYS, I AM CHECKING TO SEE WHAT KIND OF CONDITION MY condition is in and I'm not sure, not sure at all. Summer is fleeing, although the heat and the humidity cling like bloodstains that won't go away. I read in the paper that Hershey bars are being decreased in size again, the second such reduction in a year. We are beginning to worship smallness. Smaller candy bars and smaller cars and smaller families. Everybody seems to be on a diet, trying to eat less, smaller portions. We are measuring out our lives in coffee spoons. And another heat wave is promised.

The electric clock on the wall here in the office has stopped. The pendulum still works, however, swinging back and forth like a metronome, mesmerizing, hypnotic. The hands don't move. They are frozen at twenty-two minutes past the hour of either noon or midnight. So the clock doesn't work and the strange thing is that I have no desire to have it fixed. Why should we always have to know what time it is, anyway? The strange little pain in the back, between the shoulder blades, sends out a signal when it's time to stop writing and go home. The hollowness of the body tells when it's time to seek sustenance. I may not bother to tear the August sheet off the calendar at the end of the month. Fine. But why does a small voice inside me suddenly whisper, What time is it? Forcing a glance at my watch.

That's the kind of condition my condition is in. Midsummer madness, enduring August while September beckons. The ten-year-old child goes around with cotton in her left ear, a swimmer's ear, causing the ache that is like no other in the world. For some reason, earaches recall childhood and a father who blew smoke into the ear to ease the pain, and then he looked at me, middle-of-the-night encounter, strange look on the face of my father as he asks, Does it hurt much? What was that look, anyway, that still lingers after all these years? And in the middle of the night, the child weeps from the pain in her ear and we try to ease it, and she looks at me and I know exactly now what that look on my father's face meant.

Ah, sweet mystery of life that is never solved, that tantalizes us. I drive on Water Street and see the tree still there, green and flourishing, a city tree, thrusting out from the narrow alley between the Blue Chip Lounge and a weary, abandoned store, conquering brick and concrete, indomitable, defying time and the seasons. There's sweet mystery to ponder, baby, a mystery compounded of hope and endurance. All is not lost then, is it? I read in the paper that insomniacs fall asleep faster and sleep longer than they realize. Studies now show that insomniacs who claimed to sleep less than five hours a night actually sleep between six and seven. I think of all those endless nights, the sheet a shroud and my eyes raw onions, and all the time I was really sleeping when I thought I was awake.

We are besieged by statistics. A recent study tells us that the average time spent by shoppers in a supermarket is 29.4 minutes, plus an additional seven minutes in the check-out line. Why did they have to tell us that? Nobody asked for that particular statistic, did they? All the lines we stand in, all that time wasted. If the clocks stop, if we can't measure time anymore, would things get better?

I dunno. I have just learned that chocolate-chip cookies are the top-selling cookie in America. They sold $400 million worth of chocolate-chip cookies last year. This amounts to eight billion cookies. All those people sitting there eating eight billion cookies. Do the chocolate chips come from Hershey bars? Is that why Hershey bars are getting smaller? Questions, questions.

I am going to stop reading statistics because statistics also tell us how many have died and how many are not being born. The clock doesn't work but time continues to pass, and down on the street below the cop puts the ticket on a windshield because time has run out on the meter. Suddenly I am being besieged by time and my own heart is a clock. Scary. All clocks stop eventually, but will the pendulum continue to swing?

That's the kind of condition my condition is in.

August 12, 1977

"Who Are You?" Here's the Answer

IT'S THE SAME QUESTION, ALTHOUGH IT'S PHRASED DIFFERENTLY, DEPENDING on the occasion:

Who is John Fitch IV?

Is there really such a person?

Does John Fitch IV really exist?

And one letter even asks: "Why do you always refer to John Fitch IV in the third person, as if he's someone else?"

Really, what questions these are! Do I exist? If not, then who else undergoes the sweet agony of writing this column, who else is sometimes exalted and often dismayed by the words that issue from this battered typewriter, which they're again threatening to replace with a new one, by the way.

But that letter which mentions the third person approaches the real heart of the matter. I refer to John Fitch IV that way because we are one and the same person and yet we are not. He is the man I would love to be and could never become. He is a *bon vivant,* and knows the good wines of life and sips them with grace. A dashing fellow, he never needs sleep and never yawns. Accosted by a bully on the street, he would quickly dispatch him, while I would either change the subject or slip away.

You see, John Fitch IV goes places where I could never go and does things I could not do. He is fearless, except for his claustrophobia (and he has claustrophobia simply to prove he's human). Otherwise, he is a peerless performer at the art of living, appreciating all the beauties of the day and night. He never wears a hat and never catches a cold. He never gets the hiccoughs. He always has the right retort on his lips. He weeps at weddings and doesn't look ridiculous. He is a pushover for sentimental poetry and nobody seems to mind.

He goes out on a limb and takes chances on what he writes. In fact, who else would bother to write what is now being put down on this page at this very moment? But he shrugs and says, what the hell. Why play it safe? he says. Why not risk the ridiculous, indulge in nonsense? Let's not play life too close to the vest, old friend. That's John talking.

* * *

Who is John Fitch IV? A fantasy who fulfills the promises I cannot keep and lives the life I do not lead. While I walk, he leaps. Where I hesitate, he dares. Where I draw back, he plunges ahead. He sends old-fashioned valentines with sweet verses and lets others send those sleek contemporary types. He orders daisies for a bouquet in February, which is the wrong month, probably. But aren't daisies more beautiful in the starkness of February? Things out of season, that's what John Fitch IV wants. Christmas in July and Easter in January. Why not?

John Fitch IV is my alter ego and together we indulge in a sweet schizophrenia.

And who am I? His custodian, his guardian, his creator, with all the weaknesses John doesn't possess. But when I sit at the typewriter and assume his identity, there is marvel in my manner, and for that brief time I, too, am untouched by error, and I am forever young and gallant, and age has no hold on me and even my weaknesses are blessed with benevolence.

Enough of this madness.

July 16, 1971

Movies,
Books, and
Others

The Movie Talker

I CAN'T STAND PEOPLE WHO TALK AT THE MOVIES. I DON'T MEAN PEOPLE WHO make a remark or two once in a while. In fact, that's what's enjoyable about going to the movies with someone—it's good to have another person along to point out one thing or another, to share a brilliant scene or a marvelous moment of acting.

No, I mean the people who keep up a constant commentary on what's happening on the screen, in scene after scene. Or those people who, so help me, give advice to the actors and actresses, warning them, scolding them, praising them, and talking as if the screen characters can actually hear them and are able to respond.

The other night I saw *The Towering Inferno* and I ended up sitting beside two women. They were probably in their late thirties or early forties.

As soon as the film started, I knew that I was in for an evening of chatter and comment. I contemplated moving to another seat, but the theater was pretty crowded and I figured they'd settle down after a while.

But they didn't. In fact, the comments during the Coming Attractions were just a warm-up for the feature movie itself.

I realized after a while that both women weren't talking. Only one of them, the one in the seat next to me, was carrying on the commentary. And the commentary turned out to be either a remark about the action or direct advice to the actors and actresses, sort of like an extra sound track. The talker's companion seldom said anything, but when she did it was usually a murmur of agreement.

Seldom did a scene pass without comment.

For instance, early in the film, fire bursts out in a storage area and the flames begin to spread, unseen, behind closed doors. Now, everyone knows that if you open a window or a door, that rush of air will feed the flames. So here we have the fire going on behind a door and, sure enough, along comes an actor who suspects something is wrong but isn't quite sure what it is.

The woman in the next seat carried on like this:

"Oh-oh.

"He's gonna open that door.

"I know he's gonna open that door.

"And you know what's gonna happen.

"Look, he's getting closer.

"I hope he doesn't open it.

"Hey, don't open that door.

"Can't you smell the smoke?

"Feel the door, feel it, see if it's hot.

"He's not gonna feel it.

"He's gonna open that door . . ."

And all the time, I'm watching the scene and listening to the woman, and, I don't know, she's got me all concerned and worked up about the situation.

The actor opens the door—and there's a whoosh of flame.

"See? I knew he shouldn't have opened that door. But he had to open it . . ."

And off we went to another scene.

She wasn't talking very loud, really, just above a whisper. And, frankly, there was so much sound and fury on the screen that I don't think her voice carried very far.

After a while I began to enjoy her comments. When Fred Astaire made his entrance, she said:

"Isn't he a terrific walker? I love to see him walk."

I almost agreed with her out loud because I've always thought Astaire walked just as beautifully as he danced.

The woman also injected her own element of suspense into the movie. Mostly by wrong guesses. When Astaire first appeared, she said: "I'll bet he plays the part of the senator." He didn't.

Along the way, I picked up quite a bit of information about the plot and the actors and actresses. She reported that Paul Newman drinks about two cases of beer every day but looks marvelous and that Steve McQueen is breaking up with Ali MacGraw. Stuff like that.

Now, if the picture had been anything but *The Towering Inferno*, I'd have changed seats in the first five minutes or so. But action and disaster were the keynotes of the movie, and with all that action going on the whispered words of the woman beside me were mild. You didn't have to ponder the dialogue or grope for meanings—*The Towering Inferno* sets out to grip you with its flames and searing deaths and narrow escapes, and after a while you become numb. After a while I also started to depend on the woman's remarks.

When the scenic elevator begins its perilous descent as flames eat away at the building and explosions rock the elevator, her comments were soothing.

"They're gonna be all right," she said. "I know it. They're gonna make it. Watch and see . . ."

When the movie, which, incidentally, has more excitement and tragedy and awesome special effects than any movie I remember—making Clark Gable's *San Francisco* seem pale by comparison—anyway, when the movie ended and the lights came up I almost leaned over to the woman to thank her for an enjoyable evening.

And I was tempted to ask her to meet me at the theater when *Earthquake* arrives. . . .

January 21, 1975

The Film Fan

THE TRUE FILM FAN HAS CERTAIN PECULIARITIES THAT AMOUNT TO OBSESSION. For instance, if you are really crazy about movies, it's absolutely necessary to see the movie from the beginning. Arriving late, even by a few seconds, is heart-wrenching. It means there is no choice but to leave, to come back some other time, the next showing or the next night.

Another thing the film addict finds necessary for complete satisfaction is the marvel that is known as Coming Attractions. These trailers, as they are known in the trade, are beautiful. They are filled with promises—promises of action and romance and mystery. They are the sweet tease, the dangling of delicious bait, the come-hither hint of future delights.

A visit to the movies without those tantalizing trailers leaves the aficionado curiously unfulfilled, unsatisfied.

"Don't brood," she says, when the feature splashes on the screen without any Coming Attractions preceding it. "Maybe they'll show them later."

But in your heart you know they won't.

Then the thought occurred: Am I alone in this aberration? Is there something peculiar about me because I often find that the coming attractions are better than the feature presentation? Am I at odds with even other film addicts because one of my fondest dreams is an evening filled with nothing but coming attractions?

That's why it was sweet to learn in the *New York Times* that trailer addicts actually exist and, in fact, there are at least six thousand such persons in Los Angeles alone. Recently, the Los Angeles County Art Museum presented three hours and forty-five minutes of coming attractions and the place was sold out. The addicts watched eighty-three separate bits of film selling eighty-three movies, everything from The Most Eagerly Awaited Picture in the History of Film *(Gone With the Wind)* to The Strangest Story the Screen Has Ever Known *(Devil Doll)* —although it could have been a thousand others).

Ah, those trailers. What bliss they brought and what anguish they caused when we were much younger, sweetheart. It was a project to get to the movies in those days because a Depression kid had to sell empty pop bottles or run a thousand neighborhood errands to scrape up the admission fee to that Saturday afternoon movie. Once there, however, we had much to feast upon. Movietone News ("The Eyes and Ears of the World"—or was that Pathe?)—anyway, the newsreel and a Looney Tune cartoon or a Pete Smith Specialty maybe, and then the co-feature *(Charlie Chan's Secret,* starring Warner Oland), the Prevues of Coming Attractions, and, finally, the feature attraction *(Angels With Dirty Faces,* starring James Cagney and Pat O'Brien). But wait, reverse the film, because suddenly our hearts are back there in the coming attractions. We were tantalized with scenes from a movie of such heroic proportions ("Adventure Unsurpassed . . . A Cast of Thousands") that it made us limp with longing and paled the feature we were about to see. We'd leave the theater aching with anticipation.

Why the ache? Because we never knew whether we'd see that promised film. Would we be able to raise the money? Would the vagaries of the adult world conspire against us? Would Lent arrive without warning? (As it turned out, we seldom missed a Saturday at the movies but the possibility always existed.)

Those "prevues" gave us both delight and despair, setting our hearts to beating faster, and often we'd burst into the house, exploding with: "Wait till you hear what's playing next week . . ." Hoping, of course, to impress the importance of that next movie on those in authority over our lives.

The *Times* article by Aljean Harmetz traced the history of trailers, noting the style changes through the years. In the twenties, for instance, they stressed lavishness—"Lavish Grandeur. Daring Gorgeousness. Magnificent Majesty," said the 1927 *Ben-Hur* trailer. During the thirties, the emphasis was on the word "Most"—"The Most Glamorous Entertainment of Any Year"—"The Most Eagerly Awaited Film of the Decade"—and words ending in "est." The Greatest, The Strangest, The Biggest, The Best . . . Then came alliterations: "The Mighty Monarch of All Melodramas" and "Mystical, Magical . . ." Plus the "making" pictures—Five Years in the Making. Ten Years in the Making . . .

Thus the trailers and the trailer addicts. In fact, addicts now collect trailers avidly, scouring the old studios, tracking them down when clues are at hand. The trailer for *Star Wars* was brought to the museum display in a locked briefcase and the messenger stood guard over it to prevent it from being stolen by an addict.

Meanwhile, Coming Next Week . . .

August 10, 1977

Should He See *The Exorcist*?

I DON'T KNOW YET WHETHER I'LL GO TO SEE *THE EXORCIST* OR NOT.
Ordinarily I am a pushover for horror movies.

I have been held enthralled by the pitiful creature brought to eerie life by Dr. Frankenstein and regard that scene cut from some prints of the film—where the monster encounters the small child on the lakeshore as one of the most terrible and unforgettable scenes ever put on film.

I have also had a soft spot for poor Lawrence Talbot, who turned into the Wolf Man when the moon was full. It played again on television the other day. Seeing Lon Chaney, Jr., in the role, I was again moved with compassion, which has led some people to accuse me of being on the side of the monsters.

Well, maybe I am. I learned early that the monsters—whether Count Dracula on his desperate mission for blood or The Mummy seeking a lost love across the centuries—anyway, they are all pathetic creatures and they are usually driven to violence by men who are trying to exploit them. Or who don't understand the fuse that drives them.

But *The Exorcist* is another thing altogether.

I first learned of the novel in trade journals long before it was published and I read it as soon as it was issued. The book was spellbinding, a horror story in the full sense of the word. It's this kind of novel: You keep hearing odd, elusive noises somewhere in the house while reading it and you also have to keep telling yourself that, after all, it's only fiction, in order to hold off impending panic.

And then, a few nights after I had finished the novel, I tuned in to a late-night talk show on television and there was William Peter Blatty, the author. And he gave credence to some of the rumors I'd heard—that the novel was based on an actual case.

This shot down my only defense.

It's common knowledge now that Blatty used an actual case, and there have been all those stories about the movie and the faintings and panicky calls to priests by people who had seen the movie.

But I read the novel at a time when very few other people had done so and little was known about its origin.

And there I was at almost one o'clock in the morning, sitting up alone and learning from the author that no, this wasn't completely fiction. It had happened.

The thrill of being scared in a movie or while reading a book is based on the fact that you are sitting there safely. The movie ends and you step out of the theater and the safe, ordinary world surrounds you. Or you close the book and shut the door on a world alien to yours.

But when the horror can rise from the page or the screen, that's a different situation.

The night I heard Blatty on television, I felt like a kid again in the days when the night held unknown terrors. I sat up awhile in the den and heard the clock strike two. Frankly, I was scared stiff. And this was strange because I am a night person. For many years I worked the night beat and two o'clock in the morning has always been as familiar to me as two in the afternoon. But that night, I made my way to bed while glancing over my shoulder. Honest. I told myself to be reasonable, that it was ridiculous to get upset about a book. It took a long time to fall asleep.

*   *   *

And now the movie is here and I've watched more talk shows and have seen interviews with the girl who plays Regan and the others, and have read the reviews and the articles. I read an interview yesterday in which a priest—described as a 200-pound six footer—admitted screaming during the film.

What's happened is that the movie has become that rare thing—a phenomenon in itself, a part of our lives and not simply a part of our culture.

What I mean is this: the movie is an event, a happening, it is no longer simply a motion picture but has a life of its own. And I think it's almost impossible to view it simply as a film now—you have to take to the theater all your preconceptions, all the knowledge of the articles and talk-show conversation and photos you've encountered.

And that's why I may not go to see it.

It's not because I'm scared.

No.

Of course not.

After all, it's only a movie.

Isn't it?

Well, isn't it?

February 14, 1974

Since *The Exorcist*

SOME STRANGE THINGS HAVE BEEN HAPPENING SINCE I SAW *THE EXORCIST.*

First of all, I arrived home from the movie to find that the garbage disposal had gotten jammed. Now, this only happens two or three times a year. And why should it have occurred the day I saw the movie? The repairman who fixes the thing usually shows up in a couple of hours but this time it took him two days. What stopped him anyway?

Now, ordinarily when the disposal unit jams, there's a perfectly logical explanation. Last time, part of a small skewer got stuck in the thing. But this time the culprit was a small sliver of unidentified metal. Hmmmmm.

How did that piece of metal become lodged there? Joe, the repair-man, doesn't know. And if he doesn't, who does?

Then there's the matter of the fluorescent light in the kitchen. It's circular and it's been working fine for, oh, four or five years, I guess.

But the other night while I was sitting in the den—this was two nights after I had seen the movie—the light started to flicker. Going off and on.

I kept thinking of the scene in *The Exorcist* where all the lights in the house started going off and on, without anyone touching the switches.

At our house that night it was only one light, and when I snapped the switch it stayed off permanently. And, as someone pointed out, the light is old enough to go on the blink.

But still . . .

And what about the dish of ice cream I dropped?

The funny thing is that I haven't eaten any ice cream for a long time. But that night I felt a craving for ice cream. Chocolate. This in itself is unusual.

I mean, before I saw *The Exorcist*, I hadn't felt an urge to eat chocolate ice cream for years. I think the last time was when I saw *Dracula*.

Anyway, I spooned the ice cream into the dish and the dish fell on the floor. Now, it's possible that I had the dish too close to the edge of the countertop. That would be the obvious solution. But I really hadn't noticed.

And who could say that it might have been otherwise?

I didn't start to put two and two together until the other morning —three days after seeing the movie—when I fell down.

Now, frankly, I haven't fallen down in years. Oh, I may lose my balance now and then but that's all. But the other day, in the chill dark of morning, I stepped out of my car, slipped on a piece of ice, rose what I hope was gracefully in the air, and landed on my back.

The car door was still open and I struck my head on it. My brief-case went flying.

I gathered my dignity and my briefcase and started to get up, and it seemed to me I heard a chuckle from nearby.

It was still dark at that particular hour and I saw a fellow walking up Rollstone Street and he might have been the chuckler. Or maybe the chuckle was only the wind. Or maybe . . .

* * *

See what's been happening?
I keep getting wrong numbers on the telephone.
Either that, or the line is busy.
I've lost my appetite for pea soup.
The electric light bill came and it's never been so high.
I almost ran out of gas last week.
My briefcase again opened accidentally one day.
There was no heat in the office one morning.
I'll tell you one thing—if they make a sequel to *The Exorcist*, I'm staying home.

February 26, 1974

Little Orphan Annie Is Dead

LITTLE ORPHAN ANNIE IS DEAD.
    She died quietly at the age of fifty-two in the office of the New York *Daily News*.
    Someone closed her fried-egg eyes and pulled the plug on the electric current that frizzled her hair.
    She leaves her father, Daddy Warbucks, some old friends like Punjab, and her pal, Sandy, who never learned to bark but always said simply "Arf." Or sometimes "Arf, Arf."
    She also leaves millions of kids who drank gallons of Ovaltine in order to obtain that special mug engraved with her picture, or the other Little Orphan Annie souvenirs, like code rings and such.
    It's kind of sad, of course.
    It's sad because her death heralds the end of an era. I mean, if Little Orphan Annie is mortal, then can our other old favorites be safe?
    Does this mean that the Phantom *(The Ghost Who Walks)* is doomed? That Brenda Starr is in danger before the honeymoon is over?
    Actually, Annie died of premature old age. Back in 1931, surveys of the funny pages (as they were called then) showed her to be vigorous and in perfect health. But in recent years her popularity has sagged. A while back, her editors tried an emergency operation, reprinting some

of the old panels from her heyday. But the series has now been con-
cluded with no sign of new life. And Annie has reached the end of the
road.

I feel kind of guilty, though. There was a time when the events in
the funnies stirred my boyhood imagination and thrilled me endlessly.

I remember when Brick Bradford was miniaturized and set into
that spot near Abe Lincoln's nose on the Lincoln penny and began
his marvelous adventures in a new world.

And who can forget, of course, that visitor from the planet Kryp-
ton who made his appearance in Action Comics and stayed to become
one of the greatest heroes of all—Superman?

Even Beth, that lovable Big Sister of Buddy and Donny, kept us
guessing day by day, wondering what would happen next.

And does anybody remember a character named Ben Webster? (He
must have shuffled off this mortal coil years ago, because I only draw
blanks when I mention his name.)

Ah, they were marvelous, all of them—the funny ones like Mutt
and Jeff, and Dagwood and Blondie and Li'l Abner, as well as the
heroes like Terry and the Pirates with the Dragon Lady lurking
nearby.

Dick Tracy and all the gang, and how we were all in love with Tess
Trueheart. What a name and what a girl! Ah, Tess, who can ever
forget you?

Those old comics were drawn with tender loving care by artists like
Chester Gould and Milton Caniff. And the plots were daring and
imaginative. I remember a Dick Tracy plot in which it was impossible
to track down the killer because all the victims appeared to be shot
but no bullet could be found in the bodies. This puzzled us for weeks
and was the topic of those street corner conversations that passed the
time as we watched the girls go by.

Finally Tracy solved the crime—the bullets were made of ice! They
melted, of course, after killing the victim, leaving no clue behind.

Beautiful.

Strangely enough, I ran across this plot years later in a crime novel
—but Chester Gould and Dick Tracy were on the scene first.

*   *   *

Anyway, anyway.

I feel guilty about Little Orphan Annie's death and the possible departure of others, because I have been unfaithful to them for many years.

There came a time when the enchantment of the comics paled and I left my old friends behind. Oh, I had a feeling they were still there, that Etta Kett was still flirting with all the boys and Skeezix was aging gently in Gasoline Alley and Prince Valiant was still riding his horse through pages of history.

I get a kick out of some of the new comics—the assorted characters in Peanuts who are impossible to resist, for instance—but it isn't the same, somehow, not the same at all.

I think of that lost boy who waited every evening for the papers to come and then turned to the funny page first of all to see what happened next.

Now he turns to other pages to see what happens next—and finds out that Little Orphan Annie is dead.

Good-bye, Annie.

March 5, 1976

Nostalgia's Magic at Work

IS IT POSSIBLE TO FEEL NOSTALGIA FOR A TIME AND A PLACE YOU'VE NEVER known, streets you never walked, and buildings you've never entered? Of course, of course. I have never, for instance, visited Paris and yet am constantly beckoned back to that city and the bistros and the Left Bank and the sidewalk cafés where Hemingway and Fitzgerald sat and drank away the afternoons, the Paris to which James Baldwin fled, the Paris of Gertrude Stein and Sartre and all the sad young men and women of a lost generation, Jake Barnes and Lady Brett and the heartbreaking taxi ride, and isn't it pretty to think so?

Nostalgia is not what it used to be, they say. And of course it isn't. Nostalgia today has become a business and thus its sweet, sad edge is blunted. Manufactured nostalgia loses its power to move the soul, to sting the memory. For instance, the Ed Sullivan show the other night was marvelous in many ways, bringing back glimpses of people, their songs and dances and old jokes, but while we laughed and made merry when Jackie Gleason's Poor Soul chased the cakes, we weren't really victimized by true nostalgia. For one thing, the events moved too quickly and we were not allowed to indulge in reminiscences.

Nostalgia is the unexpected evocation of another time and place. It's switching channels on television on a Sunday afternoon and coming upon the final scene of an old Gene Autry movie, *South of the Border*. Gene sang the song as he watched the girl kneeling at the altar while the mission bells told him he mustn't stay down Mexico Way. A terrible movie, really, and Autry such a wooden cardboard actor. And yet I was held at the television set, plunged suddenly into boyhood, recalling all the Saturday afternoon movies and emerging into the dazzle of sunlight with a dull headache from too much action, too much sitting on the edge of the chair, too many Hersheys. With almonds.

Anyway, anyway. What I started out to say is that it's possible to be nostalgic for places you've never been and things you've never seen. There's a new film series on Channel 2 on Saturday evenings at seven o'clock. Ancient silent films are presented, stuff we had only read about in old books on movies, great stuff like Chaplin's *Gold Rush* and D. W. Griffith's *Intolerance* and Rudolph Valentino's *Son of the Sheik*. Coming up this Saturday is Douglas Fairbanks, Sr., portraying Zorro, scratching with his sword that awesome "Z" on the forehead of his foe. Beautiful. Could anything be more nostalgic than the tinkling piano and the subtitles and the tinted celluloid, even though we were never there in the first place, never sat in those old theaters while Chaplin chewed a boiled boot in Alaska?

Thus nostalgia. Our lives are haunted houses in which sweet ghosts wander, evoking lost days, times gone. Nostalgia clubs advertise in the newspaper and send pitches through the mail, filled with gimmicks as come-ons—old-time baseball cards, for example. But life is filled with so many unexpected gimmicks, why send away for them? I can manufacture my own nostalgia, and a scent of her cologne or the snatch of Satchmo's "West End Blues," or even, yes, Gene Autry ruining a perfectly fine tune can bring back souvenirs that warm the heart on chilled autumn days.

October 19, 1971

The Next Best Seller

GOD, I LOVE TO READ. I MEAN, I AM CONSTANTLY ENTHRALLED BY THE MOVIES —*Summer of '42* and *Pinocchio* on the current screen, and I must make it to the Cinema to see Walter Matthau slouching and grouching his way through *Plaza Suite*—and television can also be beguiling—that new series dealing with Henry the Eighth and his six wives, particularly when Ann Boleyn murmurs, "The executioner is skillful and my neck is small"; and the theater, of course, constantly enchants. But really, books are probably the best of all, books that create new worlds within yourself and transport you to far places as you sit in your own den, sipping something cool in a sultry season.

It's beautiful to be headed home with a new book in hand. Something like, for instance, *The Day of the Jackal*, a first novel by Frederick Forsyth, a British newspaperman. Absolutely first-rate storytelling, that ancient art so often neglected by some of the so-called literary writers, who are too busy being cute and cunning with symbolism and metaphor to engage us with the pace that thrills. Such a pace is found in *Jackal*, although I was at first put off by the subject matter—a fictionalized account of an attempted assassination of DeGaulle in 1963. Where's the suspense? We all know the attempt was aborted, so why read the book? Answer: You read it because it is completely absorbing and takes its place with what can be called the "unputdownable" books, if there is such a word. There is now.

In France in 1963, the anti-DeGaulle military force is falling apart and has failed several times to eliminate the president. Thus, an assassin is hired and offered a half million dollars to do the job. "Jackal" is the code name of the assassin, who turns out to be a nameless blond Englishman, ruthless and meticulous, who begins to build three identities as he maps out his plans to eliminate DeGaulle. He needs a special weapon that can be disguised as something else. He requires special costumes and forged documents. He kills without hesitation a forger who seeks to blackmail him. He is a complete professional killer, going about his business with skill and determination.

As the Jackal gets ready to carry out his plans, the French police realize that an assassination plot is under way. They have only the slimmest of clues. The case is finally turned over to their best police officer—"a deceptively quiet, henpecked detective, who combines dogged persistence with shrewd intelligence." And this is where the pulse quickens and the pace accelerates. The Jackal comes closer to his intended victim, assuming and then casting aside identities. The rifle remains disguised—how will it be used and when? The detective is on relentless pursuit. There is murder, torture, and sex used as a weapon. The plot twists and turns. And a final confrontation brings the book to a soaring, searing climax. Beautiful. Not great writing but great storytelling.

What is the special magic that creates those books that can't be put down? Sometimes they're crude, like *The Postman Always Rings Twice,* or underrated, like Ed McBain's 87th Precinct series, but they keep us up beyond midnight. At the moment, two horror novels are tenants of the best-selling list, but while *The Other* can be set aside for a day or two, *The Exorcist* is, well, unputdownable, until the last page is turned. *The Godfather* was hammered out in prose that often lacked grace, but what a magnificent story Mario Puzo told. Incidentally, Atheneum, which published his first novel, turned down *The Godfather,* but Putnam picked it up. Probably too down-to-earth for Atheneum, which gives us such too-precious stuff as Reynolds Price's *Permanent Errors.* Now Mario Puzo is writing a sequel to *The Godfather* and more storytelling magic awaits.

Yes, the books, the books. Fine dear things to have around the place. Books from other seasons to be enjoyed constantly—Brian Moore's *The Lonely Passion of Judith Hearne* and Saroyan's early stuff, to say nothing of Thomas Wolfe. Special favorites like *Conversations With Nelson Algren* and Ferlinghetti's *A Coney Island of the Mind.* Give me midnight and the house quiet and a book. The Jackal on the move, getting closer, closer to his quarry . . . One could do worse than be a reader of books.

August 10, 1971

The Days of Sweet Innocence

THE MOVIES, BLESS THEM, WERE SO INNOCENT IN THOSE DOUBLE-FEATURE days that they left an imprint upon an entire generation. For instance, they led us to believe that:

The good guy always wins out in the end.

And walks off into the sunset with the beautiful girl.

You were sure to win the fight—or the war—because you were on the side of right.

The villains all wore mustaches.

And were dressed in black.

The family doctor always had white hair.

And made house calls.

While every lawyer wore a vest.

A girl was plain and dowdy with glasses on—but as soon as she took them off, she became beautiful.

And a fellow wearing glasses was either a weakling or a sissy.

The movies in their naive wisdom taught us many things. For instance, that:

You can always cut them off at the pass.

Everyone dies with a memorable message on their lips.

The cavalry always arrives in the nick of time.

And the governor never fails to call from his mansion minutes before the execution.

Political candidates make speeches only on the rear platforms of trains.

And time passes by like the leaves of a calendar torn off by invisible hands.

Even if your football team is weak and helpless, a locker room speech by the coach will turn the tide.

The surgeon starts off each operation by saying: "Scalpel please."

The enemy airplanes always make an angry buzzing sound, but the American planes sound low and deep and somehow noble.

Ah, how many times we emerged from the darkened theater, blinking our way into the afternoon sunlight, believing that:

All librarians were spinsters.

Chambermaids were always French.

Every cop had a brogue.

Every private eye has a wise-cracking secretary who secretly loves him.

The cowboy's hat never falls off in a fight.

If you put on a tuxedo, you can immediately start dancing like Fred Astaire.

Every floorwalker in a department store wears a boutonniere.

And every pirate wears an eye patch.

London is always foggy and they play darts in every pub.

The understudy always stops the show when she goes on in place of the star.

Reporters wear their press passes tucked into their hatbands.

And managing editors call out "Stop the presses."

There's a guy from Brooklyn in every army platoon.

And a heel always throws himself upon the hand grenade to save lives in the big battle.

New York cab drivers never hesitate when they're told to "Follow that car."

If an actor suddenly coughs, it means he is doomed to die soon.

From some disease that's never identified.

An unseen hand always cuts the telephone wire when the pretty young thing is trying to call the police.

When you fall in love, music starts playing.

Even if you're in the middle of nowhere.

How the movies enchanted us with such innocence, and yet we know better now, don't we? We've learned that you don't always walk off into the sunset and taking off your glasses is no guarantee of beauty and the good guy doesn't always win—although it was marvelous to believe so for a little while, once upon a lovely time.

October 22, 1973

The Spectators and Some Magazines

AS WE CONTINUE OUR PURSUIT OF COOL, WE MIGHT CONSIDER THE SPECTATOR who also serves while he only stands and waits, and how many of us are the witnesses and not the participants. So many of us are members of a wistful audience, having never hit a home run or scored a touchdown or rescued a maiden in distress or cornered the bad guy in an alley. Yet in spirit we have done so as we leap to our feet in the stadium or sit enthralled in the darkened theater or even while slouched on the sofa in front of the television set. And even this passive position can be turned into a thing of cool if you are a poet, either of words or of the spirit.

James Dickey is both. He has written some of the most remarkable poems of this generation and also a novel, *Deliverance,* which is at once a prose poem and a horror story, the horror exploding suddenly after pages of quiet menace. As a poet, he has now written a marvelous poem on an unlikely subject and it appears in the September *Esquire.* Titled "For the Death of Vince Lombardi," the legendary football coach, it captures not only Lombardi but exactly what he has meant to all of us, either player or watcher. This is how it begins:

> I never played for you. You'd have thrown
> Me off the team on my best day—
> No guts, maybe not enough speed.
> Yet running in my mind
> As Paul Hornung, I made it here
> With the others, sprinting down railroad tracks,
> Hurdling bushes and backyard Cyclone
> Fences, through city after city, to stand, at
> last, around you,
> Exhausted, exalted, pale,
> As though you'd said, "Nice going . . ."

There's more, much more, about the man who was Lombardi and how he lived and died and how he made us believe there's such a thing as winning. And there it is in *Esquire,* which reminds us that magazines, too, can display charisma, can dispense an aura that attracts the reader. *The Saturday Evening Post,* for instance, evokes bicycle-pedaling days and a world that was Norman Rockwell, sweet, and the good guys always won at the end of the story. *Time* magazine is the wise guy, the pseudo-intellectual. Why do you persistently view *Time* with such disdain? someone asks. Because it is often so tasteless, with little respect for its readers.

For instance, its book reviewers often give away the entire plot of a mystery and can be counted on to knock a book if it's financially successful. One of the delights of *The Day of the Jackal* was guessing throughout the book how the assassin had disguised the weapon. But *Time,* for crying out loud, tells us all in the review. Small and petty, perhaps, to carp about but a tipoff to *Time*'s contemptuous attitude toward its readers. Even *Esquire* can be appalling. In April, on its cover it proclaimed *Two Lane Blacktop* as its nominee for picture of the year, and now, in the current issue, reports the movie is dreadful and that the editors had praised the movie on the basis of its screenplay! Of all things, like praising a meal without taking a bite or judging a dancer by the swish of her skirt over the radio.

Thus magazines can shimmer with style or fall flat for the lack of it. *Rolling Stone,* for instance, can be too specialized with its articles about the rock world but can also stun with a John Lennon interview or a book review by Nelson Algren, and it has an aura all its own. I still have a weakness for those brief jokes at the end of *Reader's Digest* articles and for *New Yorker* cartoons, although its precious writing turns me off on occasion. And I can't wait to read in book form Pauline Kael's dissertation on *Citizen Kane,* which I missed in *The New Yorker,* where it appeared originally. Oh, yes, and then there's— but enough, enough. We began in search of cool and lost ours, but will continue the pursuit another day.

August 26, 1971

Many Farewells—A Summer Voice

HERE TODAY AND GONE TOMORROW AND HOW WE SHUFFLE OFF THIS MORTAL coil, and it's all so sad, so sad. Reading Bennett Cerf's obituary in the Sunday *Times* brought back the echoes of his outrageous puns and how he managed to publish William Faulkner and John O'Hara—

how marvelous those Thanksgiving evenings were when the new
O'Hara novel was opened, because Random House issued O'Hara on
the Thanksgiving Day holiday for years and years—anyway, Bennett
Cerf gave us so much laughter and literature, a beautiful combination, and that doesn't even include his appearances on *What's My
Line*, which I seldom watched. Now O'Hara is dead, too, having kept
his own appointment in Samarra.

There's a chilling line in the *Times*'s obituary. Speaking of Cerf's
delight in his job, the obit goes on: " 'I have enjoyed every moment
of it,' he [Cerf] said in an interview for this article," the article, of
course, being Cerf's own obituary. I have written before of the new
policy of the *Times* by which obits are not only prepared in advance—
standard policy on most newspapers—but the subjects actually inter-
viewed. Alden Whitman, who writes most of the obits, collected a
series of them in a marvelous volume called, obviously, *The Obituary
Book*, and it makes fine reading, all those vivid biographies. But coming across the practice in an actual obit on page 56 of the *Times* gives
us a sudden awareness of death and loss.

Bennett Cerf probably would not want to leave a chill on the evening air, even in his own obituary. Not the man who loved puns and
shaggy-dog stories the way he did. Cerf was a publisher of the first
rank—bringing to the public such disparate talents as William
Saroyan and James Jones—and he was a raconteur and a television
personality and he gave wonderful dinner parties—"It's Bennett's the-
ory," his wife said, "that if you're going to have two people for dinner, you might as well have forty"—and he wrote columns for the
Saturday Review and syndication, but he warms the heart because of
his weakness for ridiculous jokes. I mean, who can resist a man who
tells of a maker of eyeglasses who has moved his shop to an island off
Alaska and is now known as an optical Aleutian?

Bennett Cerf also dealt with death in his many books and compila-
tions of humor, but looking always on the bright side. He reported
on epitaphs dreamed up by various celebrities, such as W. C. Fields:
On the whole I'd rather be in Philadelphia; Lionel Barrymore: Well,
I've played everything but a harp; Paul Whiteman: Gone to look for
the lost chord; Dorothy Parker: Excuse my dust. And that remarkable
and moving epitaph that Ben Franklin suggested for his own tomb-
stone:

The body of
Benjamin Franklin, printer,
(Like the cover of an old book,
Its contents torn out,
And stript of its lettering and gilding)
Lies here, food for worms!
Yet the work itself shall not be lost,
For it will, as he believ'd, appear once more
In a new
And more beautiful edition,
Corrected and amended
By its Author!

Yes, it's sad to pick up the paper day after day and read of the departures. Bennett Cerf one day and Ted Lewis another. Ted Lewis and the battered top hat and his shadow and his eternal question: "Is Everybody Happy?" Eighty years old and he hadn't made a public appearance for six years but he did not consider himself retired. How can you retire from something you love? Those who are of a certain age remember when he appeared at the Plymouth Theater in Worcester, wielding the clarinet and floating across the stage:

And when it's twelve o'clock,
We climb the stair,
We never knock
For nobody's there. . . .
Just me and my shadow . . .

Poignancy on the stage, and the amazing part of it all is that some remember him from as long ago as 1911 and others as recently as the early 1960s.

As long as we are so preoccupied by death today, we might as well ponder another kind of death, the going of August, which always signifies summer's sad departure, farewell to the long, languid days and firefly evenings, walks on the beach early in the morning mist, stilled Sunday afternoons downtown, and a walk at dusk along Mirror Lake at Coggshall Park. And a voice calling in the distance: "Jimmy, Jimmy . . ." the voice of a girl, perhaps, or a child, rising on the evening air. "Jimmy, Jimmy . . ." And finally the answer: "Here I am, over here . . ." Ghostly voices across the water—who was Jimmy, anyway, and who was calling him? Our lives are filled with small unsolved mysteries, answers to questions we never learn, and I still hear that small voice, a mystery that is part of summer, which in itself, of course, is a mystery.

August 31, 1971

Happily Ever After?

DID THEY REALLY LIVE HAPPILY EVER AFTER?

Or did they live out their lives in cushioned hells?

Or lead Thoreau's life of quiet desperation?

What happened, for instance, to Frederic Henry after he walked back to that hotel in the rain following Catherine's death in childbirth?

Hemingway himself couldn't make up his mind. He wrote, oh, twenty or thirty versions of that last chapter of *A Farewell to Arms,* taking Frederic Henry beyond the rain and beyond the years, but finally dropping it all in favor of that brief and eloquent but shattering last line.

So we conjecture. Frederic Henry, if he had lived, would be an old man by now, in his late seventies perhaps. Would the memory of that retreat at Caporetta have remained with him all these years? And would he have married eventually, after the anguish of Catherine Barkley's death had diminished? Who knows? Who knows?

The point of it is that some writers have created characters who are so vivid with life upon the page that they virtually spring into reality and remain with us for a long time.

Take Holden Caulfield, for instance, that ancient child of sixteen who was forever impaled on beauty and waging his holy war against the phonies of the world.

Many people through the years have wondered whatever happened to Holden. Recently, Bruce McCabe in the *Boston Globe* pondered the question and, in fact, submitted it to several people.

Some thought that Holden would still be the same old rebel although middle-aged now and probably working for an advertising agency.

An obscure short story by Salinger came to light a while back in which a character much like Holden—the clues were ambiguous—died in the Korean War. It's possible; certainly the time element seems right.

But who wants to think Holden dead?

Let's think of him forever catching those children in the rye, keeping them from falling into the abyss.

Oh, Holden, stay with us forever.

There are screen characters who also continue a vagrant life in our imaginations. When Bogart as Rick and Claude Raines as Renault walked away from that airfield in Casablanca, with Bogart proclaiming that it was the beginning of a beautiful friendship, did they eventually go to Lisbon until war's end?

And might they later have opened a bar in New York, on Fifty-second Street, maybe? Or is that too mundane, too ordinary, for someone like Bogie?

And what happened to Sam, anyway?

Did he finally catch up to Rick and play that song again for him, although Ilse Lund is lost to him forever?

But there's hope here, of course. It's entirely possible that Rick and Ilse got together again, maybe, after the war. And if they did, let's hope they're living out their lives in sweet tranquillity as the days grow short in the September of their years.

To those who love and cherish books and films, the people who made us laugh and cry or ache with longing through the years are old intimates. Some are frozen in time and it's best to leave them there, perhaps. Like Gene Tierney, who was the epitome of loveliness as "Laura."

Laura was so heart-wrenchingly beautiful and vulnerable that we were awash with relief when Dana Andrews as Mark McPherson, the detective, rescued her from the killer.

And when Laura went off with Mark to, we presume, eventually marry him, it was just as well. Let's not disturb the prospect. Because, frankly, the anguish of loss would return again if we considered Laura as maybe a grandmother by now and Mark retired from the force.

* * *

They stay with us, the characters we love, and that's why I like to think that Joe is still sitting in that West Coast bar where William Saroyan placed him in *The Time of Your Life*, still sadly amusing, and helping young lovers find each other.

And although they are long dead now, let's hope that Scarlett and Rhett Butler eventually did get together, that Rhett Butler finally relented and decided to give a damn, after all.

While hoping also that Max de Winter was always kind and loving to that timid but ardent Rebecca in their life at Manderley.

It's only a game, of course, but a tender, wistful game to consider that Groucho Marx is still chasing Margaret Dumont all over the place and telling her that her eyes shine like the seat of his blue serge pants.

Or that W. C. Fields is still crying out "Godfrey Daniel" as he discovers that "somebody left the cork out of my lunch."

Or to think that the little tramp is still strutting along the sidewalk somewhere, dreaming of the girl who sold the violets as the city lights came on in the dusk . . .

October 7, 1975

A Mountain Voice Echoes in the Poem

EVEN AT FOUR O'CLOCK IN THE MORNING, HIS VOICE IS STILL CLEAR AND ringing and his mind sharp and swift as he sits at the cigarette-scarred table, pounding his fist to make a point and then pushing back an errant lock of hair that has fallen across his forehead. Outside, rain pelts down, making that mountaintop in Vermont even more isolated. But inside, it is warm and vibrant, and who wants to go to sleep? It's too late, anyway—or perhaps too early—it's that far outpost of the night when morning has already crept in, and a sort of reverse twilight exists. We have stayed up too late and emptied too many glasses, but the whole world—and this cottage in the mountains has become the whole world—is beautiful and radiant.

Having made his point with thunder, he sat back in the chair, triumphant. Someone searched for new arguments. "All right, John, how about God?" John Ciardi's eyes flashed, ready to take on even God. The arguments had continued for hours—on love and writing and money and women and work—the topics weren't important, really, but the people were, and the good talk. John Ciardi, whose poems have held us all in thrall across the years and whose essays have always opened vistas of insight, likes to argue in the distant reaches of the night. He argues the way Muhammad Ali used to fight when he was Cassius Clay—float like a butterfly, sting like a bee—that's how Ciardi performs verbally on a summer night while the rain falls and the mountains gather in the darkness.

He doesn't look like a poet, but then, who does? And he enjoys talking about money, the huge fees he extracted from his lecture tours. "I made more money in one evening than my father's estate was worth," he said. (And he memorialized that statement in a poem.) But wasn't idly boasting. There was awe in his tone—he is rare, indeed, a poet who makes money and doesn't mind admitting it, a poet with the mind of a certified public accountant and the soul of an angel. He enjoys the role of gadfly, that rapier mind thrusting always, testing and taunting, a restless mind through which images dance, images that later appear on printed pages that you can read on other midnights, still enthralled.

I recall those lost nights now because a new collection of Ciardi's poems has been published, *Lives of X,* in which the subject is mostly himself, himself as he grew up not fifty miles from here:

> Monday's child in Boston
> looked like soot on black-
> loaf cobbles under the
> screeching El On Cause-
> way St. . . .

He probes his own life with wit and candor, the people he loved and hated, his education—meeting his mentor John Holmes and Roethke for the first time. His early jobs are here and college times and the years in the service, all of it in language that leaps and laughs and weeps, maybe—obscure sometimes so that you have to grope for the buried meaning that suddenly erupts out of nowhere. These are contemporary narrative poems and he demands that his readers pay attention. But it's Ciardi, all right. His voice rises from the page and echoes the voice I heard on a Vermont mountain.

*   *   *

The temptation, of course, is to quote from his work in order to display the flavor of his talent, the aura of his presence. But taking a phrase here or a line there out of context doesn't really do the poet justice. Ciardi inquires—whether he's putting it down on paper or tossing off bons mots to tickle the ladies on the lecture circuit or winning an argument late at night with glasses clinking. A beautiful example of his approach is found in the title of one of his books— *How Does a Poem Mean?* That is Ciardian in every sense—surprising in approach, fresh in manner, slightly off-key, world-tilted. Not "what," but "how" do life and love and pain and joy mean?

Anyway, anyway. Reading his words brings back his voice, still ringing clear at four in the morning. Ciardi. And I think of the others who shared those midnight-to-dawn talks a few years ago. We were disciples to the deity we call art—or whatever. We drank and talked and argued and sang—there's always someone with a guitar—and it was beautiful. I keep saying I'll go back again to that place and recapture those moments. But you can't go home to that kind of thing. I could risk it, of course, but won't. It was a special time, a special place. But I remember. I remember what I learned from Ciardi during those mountain moments. That a poet is first of all a man. You start from there. You bleed. You laugh. You weep. You feel. And suddenly, poetry.

August 5, 1971

And So On . . .

Ah, to Be Cool

TO BE COOL. ISN'T THAT WHAT SO MANY OF US WANT AND WHAT WE CONTINU-
ally pursue?

To be in command, to have class and style, to handle the events of our lives with dispatch, to sail through the seasons of our years with skill and grace.

Coming up with the punch line at the proper moment.

Knowing which wines to order in the fancy restaurant.

Or how much to tip.

Or which door to enter.

Standing in a group at a party and saying something brilliant so that after you depart, they ask: "Who was that witty fellow, anyway?"

Cool is being master of the situation. Never a perspiring palm when you're about to meet an important person. Knowing what to say to the boss at the crucial moment. Cool is the ability to believe, to pretend. To tell yourself that you are able to leap tall buildings at a single bound, to step into the phone booth and reveal yourself as Superman, denying all the time that you are really Clark Kent and always will be.

Cool, then, is what we wish for and what we wish to be and often don't achieve. But we keep on trying—which in itself is a kind of cool.

The utmost in being cool, believe it or not, was Jimmy Durante when he played many years ago in the Broadway play *Jumbo* and was halted by the stage cop as he led an elephant astray.

The cop said: "Where are you going with that elephant, buddy?"

And Jimmy, dwarfed by the towering beast at his side, said: "What elephant?"

Beautiful. That is the epitome of cool—all the elephants of our lives lumbering beside us, our troubles and worries and woes, and the marvelous ability to say: What headache? What broken heart? What broken balloon?

There are so many different kinds of cool, really. Hemingway's grace under pressure, biting the bullet as the operation proceeds without anesthesia in the war movie. That's a certain kind of cool that's far removed from all of us. The cool of reality is the stuff of everyday life, arising from the small ordinary events.

The telephone doesn't ring and the girl goes out for a while and then returns home again and wants to ask, is dying to ask: "Did he call while I was gone?" But doesn't.

Cool is Girls' Choice at the dance and all the other fellows get asked but the boy stands there alone, keeping that terrible smile on his face like a label on a can of soup. And not fleeing in defeat. You see how various cool can be and how it disguises itself?

Cool is merely a surface thing, sometimes. Waiting for a bus but looking as if you're waiting for a taxi. Or a limousine. An attitude, of standing there.

It's forgetting your wallet at home but getting through the day without anyone realizing it.

Or having your hat blown off and someone else chasing it down the street while you wait. Cool.

It's leading the first burst of applause and having everyone else follow.

Or handing the clerk a ten-dollar bill for a fifty-cent purchase and doing it with such charm and ease that she smiles and says "Thank you, sir" with special warmth.

Cool is not passing the buck.

Or passing it but nobody noticing what you've done. But this borders on being cold, not cool, and there's a distinction.

One example: The man is cool who gives up cigarettes without making everyone in his vicinity miserable; the man is cold who constantly borrows cigarettes—or even a five-dollar bill—and makes it look as if he's doing you the favor.

But what we are interested in is cool in all its beauty, and we find it in the unforgettable cartoon of years ago depicting a man chained to a wall, his feet dangling ten or twelve feet above the floor, shut away in this dungeon, no windows or doors. And he turns to the man just as helplessly imprisoned beside him and says: "Now, here's my plan."

That is supreme cool, because cool can also mean never giving up, keeping your head when all about you are losing theirs. Cool is the constant bestowing of a certain gift upon yourself—and the gift is hope.

Cool.

Laughing on the outside but crying on the inside and pretending that the days don't grow short when you reach September.

Cool is being the ninety-seven-pound weakling but striding the streets as if Charles Atlas actually sent muscles through the mail.

To be cool! To walk with a child on the shores of a nearby lake that's easily a quarter mile wide and to have the child say: "I'll bet you could swim across that lake any day, huh, Dad?" While you evade the question and pause a moment, acting modest, and saying: "But your mother would worry, Hon."

Imagine having someone believe you could swim across that lake, courageous in her eyes, heroic, poised, not Clark Kent at that moment but a calm and confident Superman. . . . cool.

And who cares if nobody else in the world believes it but the child?

October 1972

Does the Melody Really Linger On?

THE TRANSIENT QUALITY OF LIFE; HERE TODAY, GONE TOMORROW; HAIL AND farewell; it was nice being here; the party's over; the song is ended and the melody doesn't linger on; see you later; the thrill is gone, baby, and it was fun while it lasted but nobody lives forever; and let's do this again sometime, shall we? Too much, too soon and good-bye to all that and please drop in again soon or give me a ring and please write, farewell to arms and isn't it pretty to think so, and then I walked back to the hotel in the rain.

Stick around, I may make my point eventually. Actually, what I am trying to say with other people's words is that we are constantly mindful of the transient quality of life, how nothing remains, everything changes (calling hours two to four and seven to nine), that we no sooner arrive than we are leaving. Maybe these thoughts arrive because it is January, and did you notice how the Christmas decorations were taken down so early this year, leaving our streets drab and dull? I don't know. I get in this mood and I am bothered by little things. Like letters arriving with the banal, terrible postmark "U.S. Postal Service" instead of the town and city.

* * *

Death, of course, is the great emphasizer of the transient, and who
will argue? But I'm speaking of the small deaths, the tiny farewells,
the glow that suddenly pales. For instance, how we become accustomed to things and then their magic disappears. This happens to me
all the time with music. I am enchanted by "Without You," for instance, a heart-wrenching song delivered by Nilsson, and it plays and
plays, repeating its loveliness on the stereo into the small hours of the
night. And I think: I'll love this song forever. I will be playing this
years from now. And then it begins to pall.

Why shouldn't it pall, someone asks. You've only played it, like,
nine thousand times. An exaggeration, of course, but close. Try Beethoven. Beethoven won't pall. But Beethoven is fine wine for special
moments, and I am speaking here of everyday music, simple melodies
that enchant the hours and don't interfere with other processes. Melodies that merely lilt and tilt, sparking small quivers of emotions, not
earthquakes. And so I brooded about the transient quality of things,
especially music, how pleasure doesn't endure, and then someone
says: "But have you heard Badfinger's version of 'Without You'?" And
of course I hadn't.

Badfinger on the Apple label, the Beatles' label, which meant
Beatle sponsorship when they were still together. Anyway, I played
the record and the freshness was there again. The same melody but a
new approach, new voices, a different beat.
             I can't live anymore
             If living
             Is without you. . . .
All the loveliness renewed. And then I saw, of course, that the
transient is balanced by the renewable. Life renews itself. The arrangements are different but the melody remains. The seasons come and go
but they never cease. Such a simple lesson, sometimes forgotten.

The sun sets but the sun also rises. Beneath January's frozen landscape, spring slumbers. Trite, of course, because all basic truths are
trite from repetition, but the repetition emphasizes the truth. Nothing lasts forever but everything does. The king is dead, long live the
king. Play it again, Sam. And again. The same tune but a different
arrangement. Paris isn't the only moveable feast—life itself is. Moveable, renewable. And so the turntable spins again and I've stopped

counting the times, knowing that this glow, too, will soon be gone again, but knowing that another arrangement waits somewhere, and I'm not only speaking of melody.

January 11, 1972

Tragedy's Terror: So Commonplace

THE TERRIBLE PART OF TRAGEDY IS THAT IT'S SO COMMONPLACE, SO BANAL, SO ordinary, and so riddled with the stuff of clichés.

I mean, the messenger delivers the news just as you've spilled egg on your tie.

Or the doctor shakes his head dolefully, giving the diagnosis just as you knock over the penstand on his desk.

Or you're sitting there with a slight headache and wonder whether to take one aspirin or two—and the bomb drops.

So often, tragedy comes as regular mail. Not special delivery or even air mail. No blare of trumpets.

Fate enters in the guise of a bartender or a cashier at the checkout counter or a bus driver.

Don't expect third act crescendoes. That's the stage and this is life, baby. This is here and now with no if's, and's, or but's.

I mean, there's no music by Max Steiner playing in the background.

The movie star dies, as someone says, of an Elizabeth Arden beauty treatment that went wrong, but real death is pain and suffering.

Tragedy is also the possible heavens that have been missed. The close calls.

"I was there, where were you?"

"The train just pulled out."

The deserted bus stop, the bus having departed a moment before you arrived.

He walked up Main Street while she made her way down Elm.

The telephone rang a minute after she left the house.

She went to Cinema 2 and he went to Cinema 1.

And so they never met.

The near misses.

Is it incongruous to go from the pain of the flesh to fumbled opportunities?

Of course not. Because that's the way life is.

The silly and the sad, side by side.

The tragic and the trivial.

The novelist ties up all the loose ends in the final chapter.

But nobody is guaranteed a certain amount of chapters.

You know the film will end before nine o'clock because that's when the second show starts.

But nobody knows when the man in the bright nightgown, as W. C. Fields called him, will arrive.

And nobody is guaranteed a happy ending.

Just an ending.

Memorial Day arrives and we place flowers on graves.

And stroll the paths among the tombstones.

But every day is Memorial Day for someone.

Tragedy and heartbreak in a one-column, one-inch advertisement on page 2.

"Sadly missed by wife, sons, and daughters."

The date of birth and the date of death.

And all those years between, vanished now, like smoke from a cigarette.

The voices of tragedy: "Remember me when I have gone away" and "Sing no sad songs for me." And "I have a rendezvous with death at some disputed barricade . . ."

But do those words really reveal the terror?

Or those famous last words: "I'm afraid to go home in the dark." Or, "I am dying, Egypt, dying."

Beautiful. But for every famous utterance, there are a thousand commonplace ones.

"My hand feels numb."

Or, "I've got a headache."

Or, even, "Pass the salt, please."

Such banality. And therein lies the terror.

He only went into the hospital for a checkup.

And she seemed in the best of spirits.

Why, I only saw him last week and . . .
And along came the man in the bright nightgown.

But we can still try for a happy ending, anyway, can't we?

May 25, 1972

How We Accept All the Changes

"YOU'LL GET USED TO IT."

That's what they say.

"After a while, you won't even notice the difference."

And they are right, of course. We have this marvelous and terrifying ability to adapt, to adjust, to become reconciled with our fate, to bend like the willow and not break like the oak, as Neil Diamond sings.

Things happen, both big and small, tragic and trivial, and we accept them, sooner or later.

After three days the leg may begin to itch in the cast but she finds that the situation is not impossible anymore.

He learns to adjust to that border of blur in the bifocals.

He learns to get around on crutches. Or with a cane.

We have this amazing ability to adjust despite nature's conspiracies.

The young and the old, and nobody escapes. That terrible first day at school when the child feels abandoned and cut off from home. But the next day arrives and the next. Thus we learn early that we possess this infinite capacity to adapt.

Braces on the teeth?

No more chocolate because it blemishes tender flesh?

"You get used to it." The old refrain.

No more this and no more that.

"I'll Never Smile Again," Sinatra sang with the Dorsey band. But that was a lie. You'll smile again, baby, because nothing lasts forever, whether it's a sliver in the spirit or an eruption of the emotions.

I'll never go there anymore. Yes, you will, of course.

"The next time he calls tell him that I'm not here." But if he calls, she's there. And if he doesn't, then life goes on. The sun rises and sets.

Life both saddens and gladdens us, and Hemingway tells us that we become strong at the broken places. Maybe, maybe. At least, we learn to cope, with the migraines, the blues. We are collectively a series of symptoms and if they don't go away, then we learn to endure. And achieve a kind of triumph.

At some point in life, we learn our limitations, the distances we can travel and the borders we will never cross. And we go on from there.

For years I have been haunted by words spoken by an old man in a nursing home. I had been assigned to do a story and spent a few hours at the place. I saw the old people clinging to life, the wonderful way in which some of them sat there cheerfully, the terrible way others had withdrawn.

The old man sat in a wheelchair. His cheeks sagged with age, his hair was only pale wisps. He repeated one sentence over and over again. "This isn't me." Over and over. "This isn't me."

The words echoed in my mind long after I departed and they've continued to do so since that time. I pondered their meaning. At first, I thought the man was a victim of amnesia, seeking a lost identity. "This isn't me." The cracked voice filled with protest. Words to haunt through the years.

But now I know.

Of course, it wasn't him.

I realized this the other day when I walked down Main Street in the sunshine and came upon the reflection of a stranger in a store window. You can shave every day of your life, gazing into the mirror, but not really see yourself. But suddenly in the window of a furniture store, for crying out loud, you come upon the reflection of this serious-looking man, no longer a youth, carrying a briefcase, his forehead crinkled with frown lines. No, that's not me, you want to cry out. I am Cagney and Bogart and the guy in the Winchester commercials and the man in the Arrow shirt ads. But the reflection doesn't lie. This is you, all right.

And that's when I finally understood what that old man was talking about in the nursing home. I lifted my head slightly—the dividing line of the bifocals is always there, although I'm becoming accustomed to the blur ("You get used to it")—and I walked away, not exactly sad, but not exactly in a mood to celebrate, either.

August 8, 1972

No Clark Kent and No Rescue

WHAT HURTS, OF COURSE, IS THAT YOU CAN'T INTERVENE OR INTERFERE, YOU can't do anything about the situation, you can only be a witness—and a mute witness at that—and absorb the assault on the emotions. You can't be Clark Kent and step into a telephone booth and translate yourself into Superman and fly to the rescue. It's not that kind of rescue, anyway.

What I mean is simply this. Often, you find yourself in situations where you want to help but are helpless. It can be trivial or tragic. It can be a lovely girl gliding down the street in a summer dress, her slip showing and the lace edging torn, and you'd love to tip her off but cannot, dare not, because she's a complete stranger. Or the fellow who has a dab of mustard—or is it egg?—on his face as he struts down the street on his way evidently to an important date or business conference.

Or the time during a holiday event when a balloon is suddenly set adrift and flies high in the sky while a child cries out to see his blue balloon disappearing forever. And the mother who looks as if she has been passing a very harassing day, says: "No, absolutely no. You can't have another. I've put up with enough today." It would be such a simple thing for you to go and buy the child another balloon and see his face light up, but you can't, of course. The mother has her reasons and you can't interfere in other lives, even with a balloon.

But this isn't exactly what I mean. These are the small bruises to the heart, although they can't be dismissed. Maybe I can better explain by quoting the words that started all of this in the first place, words read years ago that still haunt the mind. Attributed merely to "An Old Lady" without further identification, the quotation goes:

"Since Penelope Noakes of Duppas Hill is gone, there is no one who will ever call me Nellie again."

* * *

My God, what sad and poignant words. To be suddenly and savagely abandoned in a world without contemporaries, without anyone to call you by your first name, how terrible and tragic and lacerating in its loneliness. And this is what I mean by the impossibility of rescues. There are so many situations we can do nothing about. We see people—either loved ones or strangers—in situations we wish to alter and set right—but are helpless.

Most of the time we can lend someone a few dollars, pick up a youngster who's hitching a ride, compliment her when she wears a new dress, praise a fellow writer for a well-turned phrase, take a child on a magic tour or trip, leave a larger tip than usual when the waitress is kind as well as quick, buy a birthday gift, send a get-well card—but these are so easy, so easy.

What is sad is what you cannot do. You can't stop age from advancing on those you love or others for whom you have affection. You can't stop the years. You want to hold certain people at a certain moment of time forever but can't. Holden Caulfield in *The Catcher in the Rye* said he would love to spend his life catching children who were in danger of falling over a cliff. But another occupation also would be worthwhile—calling that old woman Nellie and all the others by those first names they responded to long ago.

July 16, 1970

The Twins That Haunt Our Lives

THE MAJOR DISEASE OF OUR TIMES, OF COURSE, IS LONELINESS. AND LET'S NOT forget its sad twin sister, boredom.

These are the diseases of the spirit, that lay waste our nights and days, and they ravage the young and the old, the famous and the unknown, those who live in chandeliered mansions and those who sit at the windows of downtown rooms, looking out at bleak winter streets.

You find them everywhere, the lonely and the bored. The man in the mod clothes sipping the martini at the party may seem to be standing still, but inside he's actually running, running, trying to escape the loneliness that hounds his life.

The loneliness haunts the waking hours—and Channel 5 is now on all night long, showing ancient movies at, say, three in the morning.

"Great," says the old guy who gets off the night shift at midnight and dreads getting home at 12:30 or so. "I used to read a lot," he says. He loved the pulps, the Street and Smith publications like *Dime Detective* and *The Shadow*. Plain language and lots of action.

But now he has television, and the flickering figures on the small tube keep him company in the little hours of the night.

One of the sad, sad sights: someone asleep in a chair, sprawled and abandoned, while Charlie Chan solves murders on the tube.

Loneliness is the great leveler, truly democratic, and it drags along boredom on its journeys into our lives.

"I'm so bored," the child says, wandering the rooms, sighing at the window, gazing out at the winter landscape of the backyard. She's tired of *Sesame Street* and the library books.

"You're too young to be bored," her mother says.

But, of course, she isn't.

The human spirit is a restless spirit, on the quest, always searching. The quest affects the old people in the nursing homes as well as the youngster who hangs back from the others during recess at school.

"Go play with the others," he's told. But he doesn't know how to begin. Loneliness shrouds the schoolyard while boredom waits in the classroom.

The unknowns yearn for fame and fortune and dream of their names in lights. And Marilyn Monroe dies groping for the pills at her bedside.

"You can't curl up with fame on a cold night," she said. And those who abandoned her shake their heads and turn back to their own lives.

Indifference feeds loneliness.

I am frequently haunted by something Nunnally Johnson, who wrote and later produced motion pictures in Hollywood, said:

"Movie actors wear dark glasses to funerals to conceal the fact that their eyes are not red from weeping."

But not only in Hollywood, baby.

How often our souls put on the dark glasses of indifference so that we don't see the despair that lurks in the everyday corridors of our lives.

What's the solution? You can join clubs and organizations and pass petitions and ring doorbells and this, too, is running while standing still.

We can resort to clichés. Happiness is a way of traveling and not a destination. Be content with what you've got. The no-shoes and no-feet contrast in that ancient story. Solitude is beautiful but how wonderful it is to turn to someone and say: "Solitude is beautiful."

Be content. Such meaningless advice for the man who opens a can of Campbell's tomato soup and watches it heating on the hot plate in the room with thin walls. Or for the hostess at the party where everything is going beautifully—they've raved about her canapés—who suddenly feels the clutch of coldness in the house of warmth.

For some reason, I think of a Bennett Cerf fable that deals with warmth and cold and one of the seasons of the soul. It doesn't have anything to do with loneliness—or does it?

It concerns the poor but loving mother living in a hovel without any money, not even enough to buy a blanket for her small son. To shelter him from the biting cold and even the snow that sifts through the cracks of the sagging hut, she covered him with boards and driftwood.

One night, the boy wrapped his arms around his mother and murmured with contentment: "Mom, what do poor people do on cold nights like this, who have no boards or driftwood to put over their children?"

Maybe the answer is somewhere in that story, after all.

February 8, 1973

Keep the Faith, Baby

KEEP THE FAITH, BABY, THEY SAY. AND WE KEEP IT, ALTHOUGH THERE'S BOTU-lism in the soup and mercury in the fish and metal in the cereal and even some Pepsi-Cola has been contaminated—which makes television's Pepsi generation a sad thing, suddenly—and pollution assails our eyes and lungs and nostrils and the rivers still slither like foul snakes through our towns and cities while soot stains the buildings and roofs, but yes, baby, we're keeping the faith.

We are in the age of anxiety and the age of the ugly. You can't tell the boys from the girls, and if a certain style diminishes the delights of a girl's face and figure, then the designers conjure it into existence. We are in the age of the pill and the syringe, and the tranquilizers and the ups and the downs. The children have tracks in their arms and anguish in their souls and nightmares in their sleep, and they dump the ODs on the steps of the hospital emergency room and gun away in their cars. But still they say keep the faith, baby.

They're tearing down buildings and paradise is now a parking lot and the telephones go out of order and power failures darken our cities and cripple our machines. The world seems to be out of town for the weekend. We're in the age of instant annihilation. The store owner tells the customer he's all out of apple pie and the customer whips out a revolver and murders him. If the stores aren't safe, certainly the streets are perilous even at dawn, to say nothing of eleven o'clock at night. And we have to lock up our churches in the daytime to prevent vandalism and desecration.

Nobody mentions The Bomb much anymore, but, baby, it's there, ticking away, waiting for someone to push the button. Vietnam lingers. The population is exploding. Our ghettos are crowded and our highways jammed. Our cars are dented. Planned obsolescence lays waste our vacuum cleaners and washing machines. The trains don't seem to run anymore, and when they do they get derailed. If there's a corner lot somewhere with green grass growing, they put up a gasoline station. And next they'll be placing a giant gasoline pump in New York harbor as the symbol of our land. They freeze our wages, but not our taxes, and Congress guarantees Lockheed a $250 million loan but rejects a bill to provide a handful of dollars to aid helpless children.

Our buildings are burned and our police stations bombed and our universities torn apart literally and figuratively, and our parks and playgrounds are fouled and our sidewalks are littered. Beer cans sail from passing cars. Our walls are scrawled with obscenities and the alphabet seems to contain only four letters. They're nude on the stage and in the movies and crude on television, and sex is for sale in the flesh or in the pages of the books. But they still say, keep the faith, baby, keep the faith.

And, funny thing, we keep it. We keep the faith because the smile lighting the face of a child is more radiant than springtime and makes us forget the anger in the air and the violence in the streets. Dawn dispels darkness each morning in an unending miracle of rebirth. Lovers stroll hand in hand and a kiss is still a kiss as time goes by. A mother donates a kidney to a doomed son who isn't doomed anymore, and as the song says, he ain't heavy, he's my brother, and the kindness of strangers can be overwhelming. Mona Lisa will smile her enigmatic smile long after the last graffiti has been scrubbed from the walls.

Of course we keep the faith. We keep it because of another four-letter word—love, baby, love. Love that moves in our soul and sparkles our veins, that makes the world go round in delight. When love strikes, you know who the boys and the girls are. Love gives us those who build instead of tear down, who clean up what others foul, who drop in when others drop out. It's a battered and tattered planet we inhabit and our hopes are often shattered. But love is the flower that blossoms even in the dust, in the rubble of cities, in all seasons of the heart. Sentimental, yes. But no one ever died of sentiment or of too much tenderness. And if we are tender toward each other, we may survive, after all. That's what I keep telling myself as I pick up the paper every day to read the latest bad news that's fit to print.

September 2, 1971

A Small Town Called "Embryo"

"MY PLANS ARE STILL IN EMBRYO, A SMALL TOWN ON THE EDGE OF WISHFUL thinking."

There are remarks and statements and utterances and blendings of words that stun the sensibilities and bring delight, and the above quotation is one of them, a sentence stumbled upon accidentally that stops the traffic of your eyes across the page and makes you pause and reflect, and gives you that sweet thrill of discovery. This is one of my pleasures, this kind of small discovery, and the pleasure is multiplied when the source turns out to be a surprise.

Take Groucho Marx. Witty, brilliant as a verbal counterpuncher, an ad-libber of astonishing swiftness. And even if someone else wrote the words he said—as happened, of course, in those marvelous plays and movies—he brought them timing and dryness and that wild, wicked gleam in his eye. Groucho said: "Home is where you hang your head." And, of course: "I never forget a face but in your case I'll make an exception." And that show-stopper as he played the part of a doctor taking a patient's pulse: "Either this man is dead or my watch has stopped." But Groucho seemed to lack the warmth, say, of Jimmy Durante, or the compassion of Red Skelton. He was cool, antic, and a rascal.

And then I came upon that sentence by Groucho, that tragic town called Embryo and all the wistful wishes, and instantly I looked upon him anew. He is my kind of man, after all. Actually, I should have realized it all the time, knowing how close the comic is to the tragic, and how the comedians hide Hamlet in their souls and utter profundities in the guise of jokes. And yet I really can't go along completely with that statement. For instance, no matter how much Don Rickles protests that it's all in fun, his humor turns me and my television set off. But maybe Rickles has uttered words at one time or another that can stop traffic, too. Let's wait and see.

Speaking of words, what have they done to that word "like"? Such a sensible, useful word, a shortcut word, dependable, a tool, not dramatic or lovely to phrase on the lips, but so workmanlike. (But lovely, after all, when someone says: "I like you.") Anyway, along came that commercial, the cigarette that "tastes good like a cigarette should," and suddenly the word is being abused and corrupted and, in some cases, neglected. Too much has been made of the commercial, perhaps. In fact, I applaud William Morris, editor-in-chief of the *American Heritage Dictionary*, who is amused at the language purists who have kept quiet about the use of "good" in that same commercial. These are the people who insist on "feel badly" and "go slowly," and you'd think they'd campaign for "taste well." Oh, well, everyone to his own taste.

I am no grammarian and I seek words that allow me to communicate even if a rule or two must be fractured and sacrificed for the sake of clarity. But I'm concerned about "like," that old friend of mine. Suddenly people are afraid of it. They think almost any use is faulty. That same William Morris in a wonderful and lively Dell paperback called *Your Heritage of Words*—which set me off on all this—points out that even the experts have overreacted to "like" and that commercial. He tells of one editor who went through a manuscript, carefully changing every "like" to "as" even when it produced such grotesques as "he writes as Hemingway."

Let's not neglect "like." We can still say "it was like him to remember our birthdays" and "isn't that just like a woman" and "there's no place like home" and "treat him like a man." One use of the word that delights (when it isn't overdone) is when someone says: "I was, like, hungry" or "We were, like, tired." Too much of this can set the teeth on edge—the word becoming a crutch—but there are times, really, when you are, like, hungry. Not exactly hungry. But well, like, hungry. And not exactly tired. But, like, tired. Words fascinate, and certain words dance with delight. We need the rules, of course, but communication is the goal, isn't it? To reach out, to touch?

"My plans are still in embryo, a small town on the edge of wishful thinking." How I wish I'd said that.

And so on.

December 15, 1970

Sources

Key: *Sentinel and Enterprise,* S&E; *St. Anthony Messenger,* STA; *Worcester Telegram,* WT.

About the Author

ROBERT CORMIER, A FORMER JOURNALIST, IS THE AUTHOR OF SEVERAL brilliant and controversial novels for young adults, which have won numerous awards. His books have been translated into many languages and consistently appear on the "Best Books of the Year for Young Adults" lists of the American Library Association, *The New York Times*, and *School Library Journal*. Two of his novels, *The Chocolate War* and *I Am the Cheese*, have been made into theatrical motion pictures.

Robert Cormier was born in Leominster, Massachusetts, and lives there still with his wife, Connie. They have four grown children.

About the Editor

CONNIE CORMIER, WHO WAS BORN AND HAS LIVED IN LEOMINSTER, Massachusetts, all her life, has been married to Robert Cormier for forty-two years. They have three daughters and a son and six grandchildren.